WHAT I WISHED
THE WORLD COULD SEE!

OUR POWER-THE ANTHOLOGY

Vol 4

Visionary

Kebra C. Moore

Copyright © 2025 Kebra C. Moore

All rights reserved. No part of this publication may be reproduced, distributed, or transmitted in any form or by any means, including photocopying, recording, or other electronic or mechanical methods, without the prior written permission of the publisher, except in the case of brief quotations embodied in critical reviews and certain other noncommercial uses permitted by copyright law. For permission requests, email the publisher:

Attention: Permissions Coordinator
Welcome To The Storm Publishing!
info@midnightstorm.net

Ordering Information:

Quantity sales. Special discounts are available on quantity purchases by corporations, associations, and others. For details, contact the publisher at the email address above.

Orders by U.S. trade bookstores and wholesalers.
ISBN: 978-1-966612-81-0
Cover Design: Olaniyan Bukola
Editor: Austin S. Editing Services
First Printed Edition: November 2025

Printed in the United States of America

DEDICATION

To the extraordinary authors of *Our Power: The Anthology, What I Wish the World Could See!*

What an honor it is to witness your bravery, your truth, and your transformation come alive through these pages. As the visionary of this powerful volume, my heart overflows with gratitude for each of you. Your willingness to be transparent, to reflect deeply, and to reveal parts of yourselves that the world often overlooks is nothing short of inspiring.

This book is not just a collection of stories; it is a mirror of strength, healing, and divine purpose. Each chapter shines a light on what it means to be human to rise, to persevere, and to find beauty even in brokenness.

I am beyond excited for the world to see you, to truly understand your journey, your wisdom, and your power. Through your words, you remind us that even when the world misunderstands us, our stories have the power to teach, to heal, and to change hearts.

Thank you for trusting me with your vision, your voices, and your victories. You are the heartbeat of this anthology. Your courage has built a safe space for others who have walked similar paths, and your honesty will open doors that many thought were forever closed.

Together, you are shifting narratives, breaking barriers, and allowing the world to witness a side of humanity that is often unseen but greatly needed.

This is more than a book. This is legacy. And each of you is a light within it.

With Love and Support!

Kebra C. Moore

CONTENTS

Seeing Beyond Sight: From Darkness to Business Owner 2
    Before the Darkness Fell...2
    When I Woke Up 2
    Embracing the Light 5
    Struggling with Independence: The Battle for Control 10
    A Hard Lesson in Independence 12
    A Clear Path Forward 13
    Reflection 17

40-Years Walking in the Wilderness: A Lived Experience Testimony 22
    In the Beginning..22
    I Am Who I Am 25
    Walking By Faith 28
    Mountains and Valleys..33
    Thorn in the Flesh..34
    Running with Endurance, the Race that Lies Before Us 35
    The Promise Land...37

Insight and Inspirations from a Blind Perspective 45
    Life Happens...49
    A New Vision without Sight 53
    Corporate Covid – How the Pandemic Changed the World........54
    Dream Big, Work Hard, and Make a Difference 59
    Your Personal Pathway to Success..60

A World Too Bright 66
    Early Life & Diagnosis 66
    Learning the Angles of Light: Adapting & Coping in Adolescence 69
    Finding My Footing: Navigating Adolescence and Beyond 70
    Expanding Horizons: Navigating College and Early Adulthood 72
    Finding My Voice: Career, Advocacy, and Building Bridges 74
    The Tapestry of Connection: Relationships and Shared Journeys 76
    A Voice for Change: Deepening the Work of Advocacy 78
    Reflections and Looking Forward: A Legacy of Light and Inclusion ... 81
Living By Faith and Not by Sight 90
    The Journey Begins 90
    Trust Broken 91
    The Silence I Was Forced to Keep 92
    Dreams and Darkness 94
    When the Light Went Dim 95
    The Escape That Wasn't 96
    A Purpose Revealed 98
    The Power Within 100
    A Message to the World 101
    To the Church 102

Brooke Barrett

SEEING BEYOND SIGHT: FROM DARKNESS TO BUSINESS OWNER

BEFORE THE DARKNESS FELL

Coming out of high school, I was an eager young woman ready to step into the world of hair and beauty. I wanted to cut hair, color it, and soak in the energy of a salon — a place filled with creativity, connection, and the joy of transformation. It felt like the perfect environment for me. I loved being around people, giving back to them, and helping them feel beautiful and confident.

I was a kinesthetic learner — always a hands-on person who learned best through experience and interaction. During high school, I worked several jobs, mostly in customer service and retail. Those roles gave me experience, but deep down, I knew working for someone else wasn't my purpose. I wanted something more — the freedom to be my own boss, to build my own path, and to create a space where others could feel seen, heard, and empowered.

WHEN I WOKE UP

I woke up from a long dream, but it felt like I could never truly wake up. It was as if I were trapped in an endless loop. In the dream, I was in a hospital room, surrounded by nurses and people crying. I couldn't make sense of what was happening. I kept telling myself, "Wake up, wake up." The dream dragged on — confusing, heavy, and disorienting. I couldn't tell if it was real or just my imagination.

And then, I woke up.

At first, I thought it was just another dream, but something felt different. The air around me was sterile — the sharp, clean scent of a hospital. I didn't see my mom right away, but I could hear her. Her voice was soft, trembling with emotion.

"Mom, let's go," I whispered, trying to speak, but the words wouldn't come out right. There was a tracheostomy tube in my throat, and I could barely make the sounds form. I tried to understand what was happening, desperate to leave this strange place, but my mom only shook her head, tears streaming down her face.

She told me, "No, Brooke. You can't leave. You're in the hospital."

I kept mouthing the words, "Why am I here? What's going on?"

Her eyes filled with pain as she whispered, "Brooke, you're paralyzed. You were hit by a car... ran over."

Her words hit me like a ton of bricks. I couldn't understand. My mind was racing as I tried to lift my arms, to wipe my eyes — anything to bring back my vision. But I couldn't. My body wouldn't move the way I wanted it to. My eyes were blurry, and though I could make out shapes, I couldn't see her — not clearly. I tried to wipe the crust from my eyes, but nothing happened. That's when the truth began to sink in. The weight of it was unbearable. I was paralyzed. My body was no longer mine to control.

Even though my mind was struggling to grasp the reality of my new life, something inside me kept fighting. I couldn't even lift my arms to wipe away my tears, yet in that moment, I knew something deep within me had to change. The grief was unbearable, but I had to face it — I had to face my new reality. That became my journey moving forward. Little did I know, this was only the beginning — the start of discovering what I could truly handle in the face of adversity.

As the days passed — weeks, in fact — I found myself moving between hospitals and rehab centers. During that time, I began to notice something strange. When I looked at the walls, I saw things that weren't really there. Everything appeared blurry, like I was staring through a fogged-up window. At first, I brushed it off, thinking it was just a side effect of being in a new environment — this unfamiliar reality I was trying to understand.

But then, the nurses began covering one eye at a time, asking me to describe what I could see. When they covered my left eye, I was met with complete darkness—nothing but a void. When they covered my right, everything looked like a hazy blur. My heart sank as the truth started to settle in, but I refused to let go of hope. They told me, "Maybe it will come back. Just keep practicing." So, I kept trying, believing that one morning I'd wake up and everything would be like before.

Then one nurse said, "All you have to do is practice." I looked at her, confused. "What do you mean by practice?" She smiled gently. "Just try watching TV." I stared at her, stunned. "Watch TV? I can't see. I'm blind."

It wasn't until I was left alone in that sterile hospital room, surrounded by the faint hum of machines, that the truth hit me—hard. I was blind. I couldn't see. The realization was unbearable, shattering the world I once knew. The grief my mother had carried in the weeks before now came crashing over me. For the first time, I truly understood what she had felt— that same weight of loss and helplessness, only now it was mine. My vision was gone, and with it, so much of the life I had known. The very thing that once defined me had slipped away.

I couldn't even sit there and watch television—the one thing I thought might help pass the time. My mind kept racing, reminding me that all I could really do now was listen to music. But even that felt cruel, like a reminder that my world had changed completely. The darkness around me mirrored what I felt inside. I had to face the truth: I would never see the world the same way again. That realization felt like it was swallowing me whole.

While still in rehab care, the weight of grief and frustration pressed on me every day, making it hard to adjust to this new reality. I couldn't watch TV or engage with anything the way I used to, because the truth was simple—I couldn't see. I began leaving the television off, realizing it wasn't just my sight that had been taken, but my connection to the world around me.

When I came home, the pain didn't fade—it stayed with me, heavy and unchanged. I kept my distance from everyone, unsure how to move forward. The idea of finding resources or joining programs for the blind felt distant, almost impossible to reach. Then one day, someone suggested I try a program designed to support people like me—those who had experienced deep loss and were learning to live with blindness. I hesitated but eventually agreed, not knowing what to expect.

That decision, small as it seemed, ended up changing everything. It helped me realize that being disabled didn't mean living in isolation. There was a whole community waiting to support me, and through them, I began to see new possibilities for my life. That was the first step toward reshaping how I viewed myself and what I believed I could still achieve.

EMBRACING THE LIGHT

Embracing my vision was a challenge I never saw coming. After leaving rehab, I visited an ophthalmologist who told me, "Brooke, you are legally blind." Those words hit me like a punch to the gut. I had hoped—maybe even prayed—that the darkness would lift, that some miracle cure or therapy would bring my sight back. But hearing it confirmed by a professional made it real. Deep down, I already sensed it, but now I had to face the truth — this wasn't going to change. This was my new reality.

Grief and frustration hit me hard. I had always been a doer, someone who fixed things and made them better. But now, I couldn't even manage the simplest tasks. My hands, once steady and capable, were now still. And my vision—the very thing that helped me connect with the world—was fading away. Yet, in that moment of loss, something inside me shifted. I realized my life wasn't over. It was different, yes, but not finished. I was still here. Still me. And I was more than the limitations I now faced.

It was a slow process, but little by little, I began to find a way forward. I reached out to others who had walked similar paths — people also learning to navigate life with blindness and disability. Through support groups, therapy, and discovering adaptive tools and technology, I realized that even though I couldn't return to my old life, I could still build a new one. It was a different kind of vision I was embracing — one that focused on possibilities instead of limitations.

When I saw that doctor again, his bedside manner hadn't improved. I was eager to share some good news — something I believed could change everything. I had noticed a tiny shift in my sight; one of my eyes, which had been completely dark, now revealed a faint glimmer of light. To me, this felt like a sign that my vision was improving — maybe there was still hope for recovery. Holding on to that hope, I told him, "Hey, there's this change! Maybe there's some kind of corrective lens that could help me?" But his response wasn't what I expected. Instead of sharing my excitement, he gave a small laugh and spoke in a condescending tone as he examined me. "Yeah, maybe in fifty years, with some new technology or surgery, you could fix your blindness. But for now, there's nothing we can do."

I left that appointment feeling crushed — deflated by his lack of empathy and how easily he dismissed my hope. His words stung, and as soon as I stepped outside, the tears came. I felt devastated, isolated, and more misunderstood than ever. Yet what I didn't know then was that things were about to change.

I was later introduced to a community network that promised to help me. They said, "We're here for you. We'll provide resources and guide you through this." Hearing that brought such relief. I thought, Finally, people who understand. But as I began working with my caseworker, I quickly realized that the support I needed wasn't going to be as simple as I had hoped. My caseworker wasn't blind or physically disabled. She treated me as if I didn't know anything — as if I was incapable of understanding or managing my own life.

When I mentioned that I wanted to see another ophthalmologist, she looked at me like I had completely lost it. She didn't trust my judgment, probably because of my traumatic brain injury and spinal cord injury. She'd say things like, "Brooke, you can't do that. You can't make that decision."

She insisted that all communication had to go through someone else, as if I couldn't manage my own care. That frustrated me beyond words. I had always been the kind of person who took charge of my life, made my own decisions, and handled things head-on. Now I was being treated like a child, and it stung deeply.

Still, I persisted. I found another ophthalmologist—someone who actually seemed open and willing to listen. With that, I felt a new sense of urgency, a small spark that reminded me I could take back control of my journey.

When I went to see the new ophthalmologist, I felt hopeful. Many people said he was one of the best in the area, so I thought, "Maybe this is the one who will finally understand me — someone who might actually have real answers." I walked into his office with that thought in mind, determined to get a proper second opinion and find someone who wouldn't dismiss my concerns. From the moment I sat down, he seemed genuinely interested — a clear contrast to the first doctor I had seen.

He asked about my vision, my symptoms, and my history, and for once, I felt relieved — someone was finally taking me seriously. I felt seen and heard, like he truly wanted to understand what I was going through. He performed a thorough exam, and when he finished, he explained that while my vision wasn't what it used to be, it wasn't entirely hopeless. It wasn't the miracle I'd been wishing for, but it was still something positive to hold on to.

He took the time to explain the condition in detail, giving me more information than anyone else had before. He also talked through possible treatments, though there was still no quick fix. The difference was, he didn't offer false hope — just a realistic outlook and a clear plan for what came next. I left that appointment feeling lighter, knowing there were still options ahead and that I wasn't completely out of luck.

That appointment gave me a sense of peace I hadn't felt in a long time. Accepting the reality of my situation wasn't easy, but at least now I had a doctor who was willing to work with me instead of treating me like a lost cause.

After the appointment, the doctor recommended special glasses. My caseworker told me they were expensive and that it would take time for the agency to purchase them. I waited patiently for weeks, calling for updates, only to hear the same thing each time — that the process was still ongoing.

Months passed, and eventually, after nearly a year, I grew frustrated with the constant repetition. My caseworker kept asking for the same information again and again, and it felt like nothing was moving forward. I finally decided to bring in an advocate because handling it on my own wasn't getting me anywhere. Those glasses meant hope to me — the possibility of being productive again, of going back to school, of working, and living a life beyond sitting at home, staring at the walls, and attending physical therapy sessions.

After a year and a half of countless meetings with advocates and case managers, I discovered that the prescribing ophthalmologist had been a fraud. Learning that crushed me. I had already been through so much, and realizing I'd been misled by someone I trusted felt like another deep betrayal. I had placed my faith in these people, believing they would help me rebuild my life. The last thing I expected was to feel taken advantage of. It hurt in a way that went beyond disappointment—because, for the first time in a long while, I had allowed myself to believe again. I thought I was being given a real chance, a small glimmer of hope, only for it to be torn away. It wasn't just about the glasses. It was the entire experience—the poor communication, the lack of empathy, and the constant reminder that few truly understood how much those glasses meant to me.

It wasn't just about the glasses—it was about how people treated me, as if I were invisible, as if my needs didn't matter. It was disheartening to realize that those I thought were there to help were more focused on their own agendas than my well-being. But I refused to let that define me. I had to find strength within myself and remember that I could make my own way. I was done being treated like a victim. It was time to stand up for myself, seek the support I needed, and keep pushing forward. No matter how many setbacks I faced, I knew deep down that I had a purpose—and I wouldn't let anyone take that away from me.

Now, as someone newly blind, there are so many things I can't control. Sometimes I ask someone to do something for me and say, "I want it done like this, in this color," but it turns out completely different. Then I'm called bossy, or people just don't want to help at all. That's my reality now—and it's something I have to live with every single day.

STRUGGLING WITH INDEPENDENCE: THE BATTLE FOR CONTROL

It's been really hard to think back on those days in rehab and the hospital. I couldn't do much beyond therapy and watching TV. I felt trapped in my room, surrounded by four walls that seemed to close in tighter every day. Those were moments of deep loneliness—calls to friends went unanswered, and the people I thought I could rely on were suddenly gone. I was left feeling abandoned.

Now that I'm home, not much has changed. I'm still alone in a room, with nothing to break the silence except the low hum of the TV and the occasional sound drifting in from outside. The world beyond my window feels distant. I listen to birds chirping, the wind passing through, and footsteps of people coming and going, but I can't see any of it. My world is built from sounds now, and that sense of isolation grows a little heavier with each passing day.

I used to be someone who was always on the move—full of energy, running my salon, surrounded by the steady rhythm of the beauty world. I was vibrant, constantly caring for others. But now, everything had changed. The roles were reversed. I wasn't the one giving care anymore—I was the one receiving it. And that was hard to accept.

One of the toughest parts of my recovery was losing my vision. I couldn't even see my phone screen clearly or make out my mom's face. The one person I wanted to see most—the person whose presence always comforted me—had become a blur. I couldn't even recognize the color of her eyes.

It wasn't just losing my vision that hurt—it was how it made me feel small and unseen. At first, I wasn't allowed to get a power chair because of my vision impairment, and the whispers from some caregivers and nurses only made things worse. I could hear their complaints about having to push me because of my weight, and those words cut deep. I couldn't do anything for myself, and that helplessness ate away at me. I wanted so badly to gain a bit of independence—to be able to move on my own in a power chair—but every time I took a low vision test to prove I could handle it, the answer was always the same: no.

Hearing "no" over and over again broke something inside me. Each rejection pushed me deeper into depression. I couldn't see a way out, and sometimes I'd cry myself to sleep without even realizing it. The pain of not being seen or understood was unbearable. It felt like I was living in a world that didn't really care—a world that had already decided who I was before I even had the chance to prove otherwise.

Despite everything, I never stopped fighting for my independence. It wasn't easy—some days it felt completely out of reach—but I kept pushing forward. Each setback tested me, yet somehow, through every struggle, I discovered bits of strength I didn't know I had.

It's still a work in progress, but life moves on, and I still find moments to laugh. I'll never forget that Christmas when my mom surprised me with my very own power chair. I could hardly believe it. She had so much faith in me, and that gift meant more than words could ever express. The moment I sat in that chair, I was overjoyed. I started rolling around the kitchen island, bumping into a few things along the way, but I didn't care—I was moving on my own. That small circle around the kitchen might not have seemed like much to others, but to me, it felt like freedom.

She captured that moment on video, and we brought it to my physical therapist to show them. We said, "Why can't she have a power chair?" I was driving around the kitchen island in tight quarters—if I could do that, then I could navigate the world in one too. That video became a turning point, and I'll always be grateful for my mom's belief in me. She saw my potential when others only saw limits.

After a lot of paperwork and persistence, insurance finally approved my power chair. They even customized the handle to fit my hand, which had developed contractures from my spinal cord injury. It took time, but that Christmas gift changed everything. It marked a new way of seeing my own independence—no longer as something I was waiting to earn, but something I could take hold of. For that, I'll always be thankful.

A HARD LESSON IN INDEPENDENCE

Despite my excitement, the truth remained: I was still legally blind, and my vision limitations didn't just disappear because I had a power chair. One day, while in a rehab facility where everything was white and lacked contrast, I almost drove straight into a flight of stairs—twenty-five steps, steep and dangerous. I didn't see them until my nurse shouted, "Brooke, stop!" She had fallen behind, and I had no idea what was ahead. In that split second, the thrill of independence vanished, replaced by a sharp reminder of my limits.

When we got home, my mom and I had to face what happened. She was upset, demanding to know who had been watching me. She reminded me that I couldn't be independent in the way I imagined—that I still needed constant supervision. I was twenty-seven, an adult by every standard, yet that moment hit hard. I wasn't as free as I wanted to believe.

It took time, but I began to understand that true independence isn't just about doing everything on my own. It's about accepting help when I need it and knowing when to ask for it. I may be legally blind, but that doesn't mean I can't live with purpose and confidence. I don't have to hide behind my limitations—I can embrace the help, tools, and support that make life possible.

The journey hasn't been easy, and there are still days when I feel like I can't take another step. But what matters most is that I've learned to stand back up every time I fall. I've learned to lean on myself and my family to keep moving forward. With my power chair and the love of those who believe in me, I'm finding a way to navigate this new life—one filled with both challenges and hope.

With that mindset, I've learned to keep looking forward—to keep exploring new technologies that can help me live more independently and maybe even improve my vision. That's when I discovered something that changed everything: audio description. I realized that platforms like Netflix and Amazon Prime offer shows and movies with audio descriptions, and honestly, it has become my best friend. It opened up a whole new world for me. Artificial intelligence (AI) has truly been a game-changer for someone like me with a vision impairment. Having someone narrate every scene and describe what's happening makes me feel connected, included, and far less alone.

A CLEAR PATH FORWARD

Oasis Beauty Company became more than just a dream—it grew into a real business, still in its early stages but continuously evolving and opening new doors each day. Like most new ventures, it came with its fair share of challenges.

In the beginning, I faced countless obstacles. As a blind woman determined to bring this vision to life, there were times when doubt felt heavier than hope. I often battled frustration, asking myself, "How am I going to make this work?" The road ahead was uncertain, and there were moments when the dream of Oasis felt completely out of reach.

I vividly remember the early days of the project—facing challenges that most people might not even recognize as obstacles. Things like navigating spaces without proper accessibility, making sure my business materials were usable for me, or even figuring out how to operate a tablet or smartphone in a way that truly worked. At times, it felt like those small things could derail everything before I even had the chance to begin.

Still, I kept reminding myself that setbacks are a natural part of starting any business, especially one that reflected my own experience and vision. I had to push past the doubts, the frustrations, and that inner voice whispering that I couldn't do it. There were days when I felt completely defeated. I remember one moment in particular when I nearly gave up on the idea of owning my own salon. The thought of managing all the technical aspects on top of my vision impairment felt impossible. The uncertainty was heavy—almost paralyzing—but even then, a small part of me refused to give up.

However, with the support of my family and a clear sense of purpose, I knew I couldn't give up on the dream that had begun to take shape. I leaned on every resource available—assistive technology, the encouragement of people who believed in me, and my own steady determination. I started adapting to the process, using voice-controlled apps, audio descriptions, and other accessible tools that made each step a little easier to manage. Every small victory reminded me that progress was possible, and that I was slowly bringing Oasis closer to reality.

Yes, there were moments when I felt defeated—times when I truly questioned whether I could do this. But the vision of a beauty company that could make a real difference, especially for people like me who had often been overlooked by traditional salons, kept me moving forward. This wasn't just about launching a business; it was about creating a space where people could feel seen, included, and valued—a place where the community could grow together. That purpose became my driving force.

I knew the odds were stacked against me. I'm somewhat of a rarity—legally blind and living with a physical disability—navigating life in a way many people might never fully understand. Starting a business under those circumstances, knowing I'd have to figure out much of it on my own, was intimidating. But I also knew that if I didn't at least try, I'd always wonder what could have been.

When I began finding my purpose and strengthening my connection with God, I knew life would never be the same again. I could no longer stand behind the salon chair and style hair the way I once did. That realization forced me to face a difficult question: What would my place be in the salon now? What could I possibly contribute when my body could no longer do what it used to?

Others asked the same thing—especially my therapist. "Well, Brooke, what are you going to do for work?" they'd ask. And every time, my answer was the same: I want to stay in the salon. But they would look at me with concern, sometimes even disbelief, and say, "You're in a wheelchair now, Brooke. You're blind. You can't see. You can't stay in that field anymore." Still, I refused to accept that. I told them, "This is all I've ever wanted to do since I was little. There's nothing else. I'll find a way." It wasn't just a job for me—it was part of who I was. When people doubted me, I didn't know how to handle it. For a while, I sank into depression, weighed down by everything I had lost. How could I stay connected to a place I loved so deeply when I no longer had a way to contribute—at least not in the traditional sense?

Then one day, like a light flicking on, the answer hit me: You have to own the salon. Maybe I couldn't stand behind the chair anymore, but I could still lead, still create, still belong. That simple thought shifted something inside me. When I shared the idea with my therapist, I could tell she wasn't entirely convinced. But she's always been the one to challenge me—to push me to dream bigger and go further. I looked at her and said, "I'm going to make this happen."

See, I'm the type of person who, when someone tells me I can't do something, I become even more determined to prove that I can. Being a blind, disabled Black woman—if you say I can't, I'll show you I will, and I'll do it better than anyone expects.

Now that I'm showing her I'm actually getting things done—making real progress—after all the legal steps have been handled, she's like, "Okay, okay…" But she reminded me that, at the end of the day, I'll still need approval from the people who can provide the funding to move forward. And I told her, "Oh, I'll get the funding. For sure."

She understood, but I knew her hesitation came from a place of protection. She didn't want me to be hurt again, especially after the disappointments I'd faced before. Still, I had to stand firm in my belief that business must continue. Whether blind or disabled, I'm still a businesswoman, and my purpose keeps me moving forward.

Once I discovered that purpose, everything changed. My attitude shifted completely. I began to act differently, dress differently—even my nurses started styling my hair in new ways. I've always been called "bossy," but lately, people say it's gotten out of hand. I just laugh. It's who I am, and with my limited vision, I've become even more particular about the details.

But that's the difference now—I have confidence. I'm no longer just a woman with a dream; I'm a business owner. With that comes the responsibility to present myself accordingly. So you'd better believe my hair is laid, my nails are manicured, and my lashes? On point.

REFLECTION

I thank my family, my sisters, and my mentors for their constant support and encouragement. Though my vision and physical ability aren't what they once were, God has carried me through every step of this journey. I've become stronger and more resilient than I ever imagined. There were times when my vision impairment made the road ahead feel uncertain and full of obstacles—moments when I didn't know how I could keep pushing forward. But through those struggles, I found strength—not just in myself, but in my community. My family, my sisters, and my supportive network became the foundation that held me up, even when I couldn't stand on my own.

Oasis Beauty Company has been part of my vision from the very beginning. What once felt like an unreachable dream is slowly but surely becoming a reality. I know Oasis will thrive—not because the road has been easy, but because I've had to fight for it. Even on days when the struggle feels overwhelming, I'm reminded of how far I've come and everything I've already overcome.

When I was sighted, my confidence wasn't the same. I was unsure of my direction and uncertain of my worth. Now, as a woman with vision—both literal and spiritual—I have a clarity I never had before. I'm stronger than I was, and though I still face challenges, I see each one as a lesson in growth. I'm learning to fully embrace my new life, my strength, and my purpose.

Building Oasis Beauty Company hasn't been easy, but with every step forward, my confidence grows. I may not be where I want to be yet, but I am proud of the journey. When I look ahead, I see a future filled with endless possibilities.

To every young woman and man facing their own challenges, I want you to know this: your journey may not be easy, but keep going. No matter what stands in your way, you have the strength to rise above it. Your dreams are valid, and your purpose is real. You don't have to see every step clearly right now—what matters most is that you keep moving forward. Stay true to who you are and keep believing in your vision, because you are capable of far more than you can imagine.

To all the young women out there—especially those who are blind or living with a disability—I want you to know this: anything is possible, no matter your situation. If you can't see, if you were born blind, remember that you can still do whatever you set your heart on. The world may sometimes make you feel otherwise, but find your circle of support—and if it doesn't find you first, go out and build it. You're not alone. If you ever need guidance or encouragement, you can reach out to me. I'm here, and I'll do my best to help however I can. Believe in yourself, because you are capable of achieving anything you set your mind to. Keep moving forward and know that the world is waiting for you to shine.

ABOUT THE AUTHOR

Brooke Barrett is a survivor, a visionary, and a woman of unwavering faith. Her journey began with a passion for cosmetology and beauty, but in 2019, her life changed forever after a devastating accident left her a quadriplegic and legally blind. Though her path took an unexpected turn, Brooke embraced her new life as a divine assignment. Through her faith in Jesus Christ, she found renewed strength, courage, and purpose.

Today, she is the proud founder of Oasis Beauty Company, a disability-friendly, full-service salon based in Charlotte, North Carolina—coming soon. Oasis is more than a business; it represents Brooke's mission to create an inclusive space where people of all abilities can enjoy beauty and wellness services with dignity and joy. Brooke also serves as the administrator of Rich Girls Energy Alliance, where she continues to inspire, mentor, and build community among women seeking empowerment and growth.

Her contagious energy and powerful testimony remind everyone she encounters that resilience is real, love transforms, and with God, all things are possible.

ACKNOWLEDGEMENTS

First and foremost, I give honor and thanks to my Savior, Jesus Christ. Without Him, I would not be here today. He saved me, and through His grace and mercy, I have been given the strength to continue walking in my purpose.

I would like to acknowledge my beautiful mother, Saphronia Barrett, for her unwavering love and support. To my grandmother, Mae Barrett, thank you for your prayers and the foundation of faith you laid for me. To my nurse of five years, Dawauna Wise, thank you for being by my side with dedication, patience, and care. To my little brother, Nigel Bennett, thank you for being my heart and my joy.

I am also deeply grateful to the women who continue to pour into me and believe in my vision: Carolyn Covington, Monique Stamps, and Robin Adams. Each of you has played a vital role in reminding me that community, encouragement, and sisterhood are what carry us forward.

From the depths of my heart, I thank you all.

Gabriel K. Gates

40-YEARS WALKING IN THE WILDERNESS: A LIVED EXPERIENCE TESTIMONY

IN THE BEGINNING

It was during kindergarten when my teacher asked the class, "What do you want to be when you grow up?" Most of my classmates answered with confidence and excitement. "I want to be a doctor," one said. "I'm going to be a police officer," another shouted. I didn't know what it truly meant to be a doctor or a police officer. I stood in silence—not knowing what to say or what I wanted to be.

As the teacher began to look over in my direction, another classmate chimed in saying, "I'm going to be a singer." So, when the teacher finally turned to me and asked, "And what do you want to be?" I answered without hesitation, "I want to be a firefighter." I didn't want to repeat what my classmates were saying, and honestly, I didn't know anyone who was a firefighter. My answer came from the heroic images I'd seen on TV—firefighters running into burning buildings and rescuing people from the flames. At that age, it wasn't about passion or purpose—it was about choosing something that sounded as admirable and brave as the other professions my classmates mentioned. "Firefighter" felt like the right answer, even though I didn't fully understand what it meant either.

About three years later, I was diagnosed with a degenerative congenital eye condition—one that would eventually change the course of my life and my dreams. Whether it was becoming a firefighter or even a doctor, those ambitions began to feel distant, and practically unreachable. Yet, even then, I believe God was already preparing me for what was to come.

I was in first grade when my teacher noticed I was having trouble reading a book. I remember that moment vividly. I sat alone at my small desk near the window that stretched across the entire south wall of the classroom, with the playground visible just outside. It was reading time. When it was my turn, the teacher must have noticed my struggle because suddenly, all the attention shifted to me instead of my classmates.

He pointed to sections in the book, asking me to read specific sentences, and then jotted notes onto his notepad. The assessment went on for several minutes. I still remember the look of concern that crossed his face, though at the time, I thought it was just part of learning how to read. Honestly, can you blame me? The playground was right there outside the window—and what first grader wouldn't be distracted by that?

A week later, I found myself at my local eye doctor's office for an exam. That's when I was told I needed glasses. I didn't want them. Back then, kids who wore glasses were always teased and called nerds, and I didn't want to be one of them. Looking back now, I realize that moment was a small glimpse into what was coming—a quiet foreshadowing of something bigger. Ironically, it wasn't until college that I would finally embrace being referred to as a nerd.

By the time I entered third grade, my eyeglass prescription had already changed twice. My doctor decided to run more tests, and soon after, I was told I had a degenerative congenital eye condition. I didn't understand what that meant at the time. All I knew was that my vision would continue to get worse until, eventually, I would go blind. I was only eight years old when I received that news. How could anyone—especially a child—truly grasp what that meant?

Even so, I continued through my childhood, known around Trinidad as the kid who wore glasses and couldn't see very well. By junior high, my glasses were no longer helping, and my school began to worry about whether they could provide the support I needed to succeed. Before long, I was transferred to an alternative school equipped with resources that assist students with low vision and blindness.

I remember it clearly, as if it all happened yesterday—a two-hour drive north on I-25 to Colorado Springs, Colorado. That trip would become part of my weekly routine, twice a week, every school year, for five years. Over time, I came to know every detail of that route by heart—each curve in the road, every distinctive building, even the rows of trees that lined the highway. When we finally arrived, I looked around in a quiet awe at the campus. The beautiful architecture and open landscape stood out vividly in my memory as my mom guided the car into the parking lot.

My mother and younger brother looked at me with eyes glistening as we stepped out of the car and made our way toward a large Victorian-style building. I wasn't sure if they noticed, but I felt both timid and curious about what waited behind those doors. Once inside, my mother took the lead in conversation. A kind woman greeted us warmly and guided us across the school grounds to another building.

Everyone we met along the way seemed pleasant, asking the same familiar questions—"How are you doing?" and "How was your drive here?" Our usual replies were "good" and "fine," except for my younger brother, who would let out a big sigh and say, "long." It was hard for me to stay focused, because everywhere we went, I was quietly studying my surroundings. I had come with my own assumptions about this school, unsure of what to expect. So far, everything seemed fairly ordinary—what most people would call normal.

The building we entered was smaller than the others around it. We were introduced to a few more people, but my attention was quickly drawn to a strange screeching sound echoing somewhere inside. As we walked down a hallway lined with lockers, I kept glancing around, trying to figure out where the sound was coming from. I could hear voices and conversations coming from nearby classrooms, but so far, I had only seen adults.

We turned down another hallway, and I noticed a kid walking in an odd way. He was making loud screeching noises and wearing a helmet. My earlier assumptions about the school came rushing back all at once, and I remember thinking, I don't want to go here. But that thought changed the moment we stepped into the library. There, I saw another student quietly returning a book to a shelf. He walked normally and wasn't wearing a helmet, and for the first time since arriving, I began to feel a little more at ease.

I AM WHO I AM

My name is Gabe, and I was diagnosed with a vision disability known as Retinitis Pigmentosa, or RP, when I was a child. I grew up in Trinidad, a small town in southern Colorado, just ten miles north of the New Mexico border. The road trip I mentioned earlier was to the Colorado School for the Deaf and the Blind (CSDB). I was twelve years old when I first visited the school.

My teachers and school principal had told my mother and me about CSDB while I was still a student at Trinidad Junior High. But at that age, I didn't think much of it. I was young, naïve, and more focused on getting through my regular school days. Still, by the end of seventh grade, CSDB would become my school for the foreseeable future.

By the time I completed sixth grade, I was considered legally blind, as prescription glasses no longer provided enough vision correction. Reading regular twelve-point font became almost impossible without magnification, and the resources I needed to succeed in school were scarce. It was during my time at Trinidad Junior High that I was first placed in a special education classroom—a moment that filled me with frustration. I absolutely despised it. Being in that class made me self-conscious, as if my general education classmates thought I wasn't smart enough. But deep down, I knew that wasn't true. My intellect wasn't the problem—it was RP that had suddenly put everything, including my confidence, into question.

I didn't realize it at the time, but education would become a major catalyst for my upward mobility. Although I dreaded going to school and doing assignments, being in school wasn't all that bad—it was the process of getting there that I dreaded most. As for the schoolwork, the main reason I put it off was the constant difficulty of completing assignments due to my vision loss. Many of the lessons were actually interesting; I just struggled to access them easily. I've always loved learning—it's my number one Clifton Strength.

Eventually, I excelled in high school because of the supports and resources I received at CSDB. They didn't necessarily make schoolwork easy to access, but they made it accessible enough for me to succeed. My freshman year was rough, mostly because of my lingering rebellious attitude toward schoolwork, but I eventually turned things around and made the honor roll throughout the rest of high school. I was mainstreamed at William J. Palmer High School for classes with greater academic rigor, and I even took college prep courses during my senior year. While I was finding academic success in the classroom, it was my extracurricular life outside of school that often held me back.

What I didn't fully realize while growing up in a deprived community in Trinidad was how much a poor living environment would shape my life.

I was essentially a delinquent youth, caught up in an underprivileged setting that influenced many bad habits and poor decisions. It was already hard enough trying to make it through public school with a visual impairment.

Dealing with the daily challenges of poverty made it even harder to achieve anything—let alone finish high school. Thoughts of going to college would cross my mind, usually followed by a long sigh. I doubted it deeply. No one in my family had ever gone to college. Still, the lack of resources to support my vision disability, growing up in a low-income household, and living in a deprived community forced me to develop resilience that I didn't realize until later in life. Those experiences, along with the ever-supportive student success and disability services, helped me get through grade school and eventually college.

I wasn't sure how, but something in me said that higher education might be the antidote! I knew little to nothing about college, and as a first-generation student, I quickly realized that success would have to begin with the ability to pass my courses. Still, I found myself struggling to earn passing grades in every class. That changed when I connected with the Office of Disability Services. Through their support, I received accommodations and assistive technology that completely transformed how I approached my studies. I barely made it through that fall 2004 semester, but with their help, I could finally access my course materials, assignments, and exams more efficiently. By the following spring, my GPA had risen significantly, and I made the Dean's list for outstanding achievement. Around the same time, I also landed a job as an Assistive Technology Computer Lab Assistant. God was working out His plan for me all along!

When I think back to being raised in a deprived community, I often wonder what career path would have been available to me if I had stayed in Trinidad? There were no resources there like the ones I later found at CSDB or in college. Trinidad was also struggling with high crime rates, and many of my neighborhood friends were getting into trouble with the law. I had started to drift toward the party scene and bad influences, where alcohol and drugs were everywhere—partly because there weren't many safe or enjoyable recreational opportunities. Truthfully, none of them interested me anyway.

Many of my friends ended up in drug rehabilitation programs, juvenile detention centers, or even in jail. It was heartbreaking to watch that all unfold, especially because some of them had such natural talent, skill, and potential. I also started making bad decisions that led me to getting caught up in the justice system. However, because of my eye condition, I-25 North became my way out of Trinidad. It was more than a highway—it was a lifeline that led me to a city filled with opportunities and the resources I needed to achieve my educational goals and beyond.

WALKING BY FAITH

Because of RP, I couldn't legally drive. When I lived in Colorado Springs, I could use public transportation, but I usually preferred to walk. If I wasn't riding my bike, I was on foot. Trinidad didn't have public transportation, which is probably why I never grew dependent on it. Instead, I'd just lace up my Shoebarus, fire up my Chevrolegs, and start walking. I was a walking fool. But walking came with its risks. One time, I was just inches away from being hit by a train in Trinidad.

I was walking along a familiar street—the same one I always took home. It ran close to a freight train depot, so trains often stopped there to load and unload cargo. It was a scene I knew well. But on this particular day, I wasn't paying much attention. The lights on the railroad sign were flashing, but since I was used to crossing the tracks when they did, I thought nothing of it.

Since trains often stopped to drop off cargo or disconnect and reconnect to other cars, it wasn't unusual for the crossing lights to flash for long periods. Even drivers ignored them and drove straight through. As I started crossing the tracks, I noticed a train car partially blocking the street, but I didn't think much of it. That was normal. When a train blocked the road, I usually just climbed the ladder on the side of the car and made my way across to the other side.

This particular time though, I could have sworn I looked around the line of cars that stretched into the street to check for any oncoming trains. But before I could react, a loud horn blasted, I was jolted forward, and I felt a rush of air and vibration as the roaring train passed just an arm's length from me. My heart was pounding. I stood there stunned, watching the train roll past, my hands pressed tightly against my chest while the conductor yelled a stream of expletives.

Later in life, I'd come to realize it was God's angels who saved me from near death that day. If I hadn't been pushed forward, out of the path of the on-coming train, I wouldn't be alive to tell this story. . It was also God who spared my life when my friends and I crashed into a parked eighteen-wheeler at 120 miles per hour. Yes, there were plenty of dangerous and reckless adventures in those years, including many bad choices that should have had me killed. But obviously God had a purpose for me.

Back in Colorado Springs, we had what people called the Blizzard of '97. Snow piled high across my yard, turning the entire neighborhood into a white wonderland. It was that heavy, wet kind of snow that weighed down tree branches and muted every sound. My first thought was, *I wonder if work will be closed because of this weather?*

At the time, I was considered essential personnel at Domino's Pizza. No, I wasn't a delivery driver—my vision wasn't good enough for that. Just

Imagine me trying to deliver pizza and then wrecking the car into the house: "Umm, here's your pizza... that'll be twenty-three dollars and forty-eight cents, please." Yeah, umm no. My first job was as a dough boy, which meant I helped make the pizza dough. That particular Domino's was responsible for supplying dough to about a dozen other stores. Missing work didn't just mean I'd lose a shift—it meant other stores wouldn't have enough dough to meet their orders.

By that evening, the blizzard had dropped nearly two feet of snow. The local news station announced that city officials had closed the streets to all traffic except essential personnel. "Essential personnel? Traffic?" I muttered to myself, staring at the TV in disbelief. "Well, I guess I'm not going to work tomorrow," I added, realizing that even if I wanted to, no one would be able to make it in anyway. The road closures didn't bother me at all because I walked to work. My workplace was only about a half mile away—a simple fifteen-minute walk. So, I turned off my alarm, settled into my living room with some comfort food and a drink, and put on a movie. I was officially in for the night, with no plans to go anywhere.

The next morning, I woke to the sound of the phone ringing. On the other end was my coworker.

"Good morning," he said.

"Good morning," I replied.

He was also the assistant manager at our Domino's Pizza, and he wasted no time asking, "Are you able to make it into work?" Still half-asleep, I asked, "What time is it?"

"Seven o'clock."

"Yeah, I can probably be there by eight. How are you getting there?" He mentioned that he had a four-wheel drive. "Okay, cool. See you at eight," I said, hanging up. I rolled out of bed and knocked on my roommate's door. "Hey, I just got a call from work—they're asking if we can come in."

"We?" my roommate said groggily. We both worked at the same Domino's. "Yeah, I'll get ready now," he mumbled. "Okay," I said confidently, not realizing I was about to face one of the toughest walks of my life.

As we set out for work, we stepped through the back door and into the alley, our usual route.

"Dang! That's a ton of snow!" I said as we paused at the small porch, staring out at the white blanket of snow that had swallowed the yard. We exchanged a quick look before stepping down into more than two feet of snow. Each step was a struggle. The snow was so deep that our legs kept sinking and getting stuck. We found that moving at a steady jog was the only way to free our feet and keep going.

I was dressed in blue slacks, a hoodie, and plain sneakers—definitely not ready for this kind of weather. Luckily, the streets seemed to have less snow piled up, so we decided to walk along the roads whenever possible. Besides, there were broken branches littered along the sidewalks, snapped off of trees from the sheer weight of the snow.

Just about two blocks from my home, I was already getting winded from jogging through the deep snow. I was slightly ahead of my roommate, and the snow was blowing in my face. Then I heard him yell, "I can't make it, I'm going back!"

I stopped. Slowly turning around, huffing, looking down at all the snow while wiping flakes off my face, and then I looked up and we stared at each other briefly. I said, "ok."

I kept staring as he headed back the way we came, thinking for a moment if I should head back as well. But I turned back around, let out one more big huff, and kept pushing forward, desperate to reach work. It almost felt like I was living out that scene from Rocky IV, where Sylvester Stallone runs through the frozen Russian wilderness, "Eye of the Tiger" playing in my head the whole time.

As I got closer to my workplace, traffic thickened, forcing me off the street and onto the sidewalk. The snow was still falling heavily, and the wind made it hard to see. Then I was forced to stop—the path suddenly disappeared into the storm—turning everything in front of me into a blur of white.

As I tried to make sense of what was happening, I wondered, Was it just the blowing snow causing a whiteout? I blinked hard, trying to bring my eyes into focus. What the heck? Up ahead, a massive snow drift—easily ten feet high—was piled against the wall bordering the high school baseball field. That sidewalk was my usual route to work, but now it was completely impassable. I could only imagine the look of disbelief on my face.

Realizing I couldn't continue that way, I glanced toward the street. It was empty—no cars passing by. Still, I hesitated. The snow was falling steadily, and visibility was terrible. I couldn't tell if drivers would even see me, and if they did, could they stop in time? The street was normally one of the busiest routes into downtown, cars constantly flying by on any other day. Finally, I decided to risk it. I hopped down into the street, keeping as close to the sidewalk as the massive drift would allow. The stretch was about four hundred feet before I could get back onto the sidewalk. Thankfully, only a couple of cars passed—moving cautiously and keeping their distance—until I reached the other side safely. Just two more blocks to work.

MOUNTAINS AND VALLEYS

Of course, I'll never forget walking in harsh conditions like these. I guess all those days of trekking across Trinidad and back and forth to school had prepared me for this moment. In my mind, I could hear the familiar, worn-out story from the elders in my family—"We were poor... we didn't have a car... I used to walk a mile to school in two feet of snow, barefoot..."—the same story I'd hear every time I complained about walking anywhere. Well, here I was now, trudging through my own wilderness, fighting through nearly two feet of snow just to get to work. At least I had shoes on.

Walking in the snow isn't some overblown story—it's a real, lived experience. Getting from point A to point B through this kind of weather and rough terrain wasn't something I faced just once, either. Exactly ten years later, during the Blizzard of 2007, I found myself slipping and landing on my hands while climbing over four- to five-foot snow mounds near a bus stop across from the University of Colorado, Colorado Springs (UCCS).

These massive snow mounds had been created by snowplows clearing the streets, piling the snow high onto the sidewalks and blocking the very pathways that led to the building where I was supposed to attend class. I made it there, but it was a real struggle getting to that point. While I sat in class waiting for the instructor—since everyone was running late—I found myself reflecting on what I had just gone through just to get there, especially on my very first day at an unfamiliar college campus.

I couldn't help but wonder what the bus driver had been thinking. I don't recall hearing any kind of warning—no "be careful" or "watch your step"—nothing about those massive snow mounds waiting for me outside. Nevertheless, this is the story of my life: walking headfirst into situations, giving them little thought, setting out with almost no information, and rarely considering how much my limited vision could make even the simplest things harder.

You'd think I would have moved somewhere that didn't come with four- to five-foot snow mounds—or at least chosen not to walk in blizzard conditions, especially with my vision disability. Trust me, that thought has crossed my mind more times than I can count. Honestly, I do prefer warmer climates. Still, those "would have, could have, should have" reflections tend to come after the fact, when everything seems clearer in hindsight. But even if you take the snow and blizzards out of the picture, there were plenty of times I found myself walking for miles before and after work simply because I didn't have any transportation.

I remember one night when I walked nearly nine miles—over three hours—to get home after my shift at a mattress company. I was working the second shift then, and there wasn't any public transportation available that late. If I didn't arrange a ride with my brother or a friend ahead of time, or simply couldn't afford a taxicab, walking was my only option. Sometimes, I'd be asked to stay until three in the morning when the person scheduled for the third shift didn't show up. On those nights, I either found a quiet spot to rest or waited at the bus stop until the first bus started running again.

THORN IN THE FLESH

While my family and friends often asked the all-too-common question, "Why would you do that?" I was left on the sidelines, hoping and pushing for better access to transportation. I'd faced countless frustrations, most of which focused more on the problems than the solutions. Remember my coworker with the four-wheel-drive truck? He could simply hop in and head to work without much worry. After all, he was a young guy who loved four-wheeling. In fact, he described his drive to work that day as an adventure.

"There were hardly any other cars on the road," he said as we poured seventy pounds of flour into the dough mixer. "I was sliding all over, even had to drive over this huge snow mound." I couldn't help but share in his excitement, imagining myself in those same conditions—feeling the thrill instead of the struggle. Yet, in the back of my mind, I couldn't shake the thought that I just wished I had a car of my own—any car, really—so I could head out that easily.

It's always easier to draw conclusions after the fact. I mean, it's almost human nature to look back and judge situations with a critical eye, often without any real intention of finding a solution. There always seems to be this same reactive pattern that plays out every time I share these experiences with family, friends, or coworkers. But why can't I get more support—more advocacy—for better transportation? Why can't I have access to the same work opportunities as everyone else? I don't want special treatment; I just want to be treated equally and given equal chances. Still, hearing comments like, "Why don't you just get a job closer to your house?" or "Why not find something during the day?" took a real toll on my sense of dignity and self-worth. Those words made me feel shut out from a world that wasn't built for me—a world that offered no way forward, so I had to create one. Even so, I never gave in, and I never gave up. I kept fighting and pushing forward so that, despite the limits of RP, I could still be seen as an equal contributor to society—someone who belongs.

RUNNING WITH ENDURANCE, THE RACE THAT LIES BEFORE US

Blindness—or what's known as having no functional vision—struck when I was thirty-two years old. Before that, I had spent years walking and wandering through life with low vision, relying solely on memory and instinct, without the use of any mobility aids. That changed in the summer of 2010. My vision has since declined to light perception only, meaning I can tell whether the space around me is bright or dark. I don't walk nearly as much as I used to, but when I do, it's with the help of my white cane.

I still remember walking home from a second-shift job at CSDB—a three-mile journey. It was nighttime, but that didn't make a difference since I couldn't see anyway. I had my cane tip pressed to the ground—resembling a finger trailing the route on a map—guiding me from CSDB to my home. Over time, I had memorized every corner and turn of the Colorado Springs streets. That mental mapping came in handy, built from years of walking and from countless trips between Trinidad and Colorado Springs along the I-25 route. Let's just say I had plenty of time to get good at it. Looking back, that journey felt liberating. Honestly, I can hardly believe I made it.

Now, I live in the North Denver metropolitan area, where I work for the Office of Disability Support Services at Front Range Community College (FRCC). How amazing is that! What an honor to hold a position I once only dreamed of—one that allows me to pay it forward in ways that truly matter. I'm also pursuing my doctorate in Educational Leadership at the University of Colorado Denver, and I'm aiming to complete it by May 2026.

I'm not the "walking fool" I used to be thanks to Denver's Regional Transportation District (RTD). The Denver RTD program offers an abundance of public transportation and paratransit services, including rideshare options made possible through strong community advocacy and well-funded resources. My wife also steps in to give me a ride when public transportation becomes overly complicated or inconvenient. Still, I never lost my love for getting out and walking whenever and wherever I can.

THE PROMISE LAND

At the age of forty, I had a life-changing encounter with God and surrendered my life to Him. Since that moment, He has been my eyes. As Scripture says, "I will instruct you and teach you in the way you should go; I will guide you with My eye" (Psalm 32:8). These days, I walk by the Spirit, and it's incredible how much more I can see now with spiritual vision than I ever could with physical sight.

The number forty carries deep meaning in the Bible—it represents completion and transformation. The Israelites wandered in the wilderness for forty years before reaching the Promised Land, a journey that should have taken only eleven days. Their disobedience kept them wandering far longer than necessary. Looking back, I realize that if I had placed my faith in God sooner, I might have reached my own Promised Land faster. Now, I spend my days thanking God for how far He has brought me—through mountains and valleys, through near-death experiences, and through deliverance from alcoholism. He transformed me from the identity of a drunker to being called a child of God, and for that, I am forever grateful.

This is what I wish the world could see. Looking back now as a born-again Christian, I can see how God has provided everything I need to achieve both educational and vocational success—and even this beautiful opportunity to share the Gospel through my own life story. God showed me where to find meaning and purpose after wandering in this world so long not knowing what anything meant. Without God, I know I'd most likely be trapped in alcoholism, locked up in jail, or six feet underground. That's not an exaggeration; most of the friends I grew up with in Trinidad are either incarcerated or gone from this world.

Whether or not you believe in God, my prayer is that whatever you're going through, you'll come to see that He's right there in the middle of it with you. In times of pain and suffering, and even in moments of joy, God promises never to forsake us—and I can say with certainty that His promise is true! It's all written in my story.

ABOUT THE AUTHOR

Gabe is an enthusiastic disability services professional with a vision disability who is dedicated to advancing accessibility in higher education. He provides accommodations and support to students with disabilities, ensuring equal access to both curricular and co-curricular programs. Gabe's approach is student-centered—he meets learners where they are, supports their goals, celebrates their achievements, and helps prepare them for meaningful opportunities. His areas of expertise include determining accommodation eligibility, understanding disability law and policy, identifying and removing accessibility barriers, implementing effective assistive technology solutions, and applying principles of universal design.

Gabe also enjoys collaborating with other disability advocates and organizations to promote a culture of accessibility and inclusion across all environments. He remains deeply engaged in both state and institutional strategic initiatives aimed at improving equity and access for students with disabilities in higher education. Gabe co-chaired the Disability Services Advocacy Committee for Colorado House Bill 22-1225, which directed the committee to provide recommendations to the General Assembly on how to improve outcomes for students with disabilities in higher education. Additionally, he serves on a Community Steering Committee that advises the Governor's Office of Information Technology on advancing digital accessibility for Coloradans with disabilities statewide. He is also a member of Lions Club International and proudly demonstrates the Lions motto, "we serve."

Outside of his career as a disability services professional and advocate, Gabe enjoys a variety of indoor and outdoor recreational activities. Some of his favorites include hiking, biking, running, swimming, and strength training. He considers himself a foodie and often seeks out new eateries, with smoked barbecue and fusion cuisines among his top choices. Gabe also loves stand-up comedy and traveling to new destinations. His faith is a central part of his life—he spends time praying, reading the Bible, attending church, and enjoying Christian concerts.

ACKNOWLEDGEMENTS

I want to first acknowledge Kebra Moore and Welcome to the Storm Publishing for the opportunity to be part of the "What I Wish the World Could See" anthology. I appreciate the opportunity to share my story with these other courageous authors through this platform. Each author is amazing, and I am grateful to have the opportunity to join this remarkable group of individuals. I also want to acknowledge all the disability advocates and allies that have paved the way for equal opportunity. I stand in alliance with all the courageous defenders and promoters of disability rights. I want to give a special tribute to the late disability activist and humanitarian Judy Heumann. Judy was instrumental in progressing the Americans with Disabilities Act of 1990 and other disability legislation.

A special thanks to my loving wife, Gina, for supporting me through all my disability-related struggles and so much more. My greatest gratitude extends to my family and friends for standing by me and just being there with me through hard times. Thanks to all of my extended CSDB and FRCC family. My expression of gratitude wouldn't be complete without giving a special shout out, and much love to my DSS peeps, especially to my supervisor and senior director for giving me the opportunity and the honor to be director of accommodations and support at FRCC. Thanks to everyone who supported me along the way, including my mentors, those of you who believed in me, those of you who prayed for me, and those of you who gave me the opportunities to achieve my goals and reach my dreams —you know who you are.

Thanks to my pastors who gave me much needed spiritual guidance and encouragement along the way as well. Glory be to God through Jesus Christ, my Lord and Savior!

Carolyn Marshall-Covington

"With my sighted eye I see what's before me, and with my unsighted eye I see what's hidden."

— Alice Walker

INSIGHT AND INSPIRATIONS FROM A BLIND PERSPECTIVE

In the whirlwind of youth and ambition, I found myself caught in the relentless pursuit of success. Every day was a race to achieve and conquer a new goal. I was so focused on checking off boxes that I seldom took a moment to pause, to breathe, and to truly appreciate the journey. It was all about the next goal, the next achievement.

But life has a way of teaching us profound lessons when we least expect them. It was only after I lost my sight that I truly realized I was in a race against time a race that, in the grand scheme of things, was not about crossing a finish line but about truly living.

One poignant moment stands out. A doctor, examining me, asked, "When's the last time you looked up and saw the stars?" I realized then how long it had been since I had paused to look beyond my immediate surroundings. I was so consumed by daily routines that I had forgotten to look up, to marvel at the night sky.

When I finally took the time to look, I saw nothing but darkness—a stark reminder of how much I had missed. But in that darkness, I discovered a new kind of light, one not found in the world around me but awakened within. It is the light of spirit—rooted in compassion, guided by empathy, and sustained by gratitude for the moments that truly matter.

Today, I see life differently. I've learned that success is not just about checking boxes but about savoring the journey, cherishing the present, and finding joy in the small moments.

People often ask what I miss most. The truth is, I miss less than they imagine — losing my eyesight cleared space for what truly matters. Blindness took my sight but sharpened my awareness: I learned to hear the shape of a room, feel the warmth of a smile in someone's voice, and recognize kindness. I discovered that seeing can mean listening, noticing, and remembering. Join me as I trace each step of my transformation — from adapting in new ways to finding unexpected strengths. This is a story of resilience and renewal. I'll share how I learned to hold my dreams, and I hope it inspires you to pursue yours.

As a child, I lived in Glenarden, Maryland — more than just a neighborhood, it was a living story of resilience and triumph. Nestled in Prince George's County, Glenarden was one of the few places where Black families could buy homes, raise children, and build legacies despite segregation and discriminatory housing practices. It was a place where strength was inherited, not taught — where every front porch held a story of perseverance.

I grew up in a family of six — two girls, two boys — guided by parents who showed me what perseverance and possibility truly meant. From both of them, I gained a deep respect for hard work, empathy, and the belief that every path, no matter how humble, can lead to purpose.

I was a big dreamer growing up, always imagining more than what I could see around me. While other kids played house, I dreamed of running a business. I wanted to become a sought-after hairstylist, travel the world, and own a chain of salons. Success was my fairytale. But if I'm honest, what I wanted even more was hair. Mine was thin and short, soft like cat fur, and it never let me forget how much I longed for something different.

My Aunt Christine — whom I affectionately called Aunt Chrissy — tried to comfort me. She would say, "Baby, you've got personality, and it will take you a long way in life."

I remember thinking, who is she talking to? Personality? I wanted hair like everyone else. Little did I know how much Aunt Chrissy's words of encouragement would shape my life.

My mother — the resourceful problem solver — found a way to temporarily fix my hair situation. One day, I watched as she cut her own hair to make a ponytail just for me. She attached it to the top of my head, stepped back, and smiled. "Now…you have hair," she said.

That moment was transformative. It wasn't just about the hair; it was about feeling whole — because, for the first time, I felt seen. It lit a spark in me, a passion for beauty and self-expression that would shape my future.

It was 1975 — a year when the airwaves carried the smooth sounds of Tell Me Something Good by Rufus, Hollywood Swinging by Kool & the Gang, and Helen Reddy's anthem Leave Me Alone (Ruby Red Dress). Families gathered around televisions for Good Times, Chico and the Man, and, on weekends, Soul Train. In my little corner of Maryland, life moved with that same restless rhythm.

That was the year opportunity knocked loudly and unexpectedly. A student from my school was to be selected to attend Bladensburg Vocational High School's cosmetology program—a three-year course focused on hair, skin, and nail care, along with professional and business development. The rules were strict: the chosen student needed a GPA of at least 3.5 and perfect attendance. I didn't fit that profile—not even close. But dreams have a way of pushing past prerequisites, and somehow, I was selected.

At sixteen, that opportunity became my doorway into the beauty industry. I still remember the day I received my little blue suitcase—a cosmetology kit filled with the tools that would unlock my future. From that moment on, I became a mobile salon in the neighborhood, practicing on everyone I could find—for a small fee, of course.

At only twenty-one, I stepped into leadership, building and managing my own business—InFlight Hair Salon. What began as a dream quickly grew into a movement. Training, mentoring, and inspiring my staff to reach new levels of excellence became one of the most rewarding experiences of my life. The bond we shared went far beyond hairstyling; we became a family built on trust, creativity, and shared ambition.

Back then, the phrase "live, work, and play" wasn't popular yet, but we were already living that truth. My apartment was on the tenth floor of the prestigious Park Place Towers at 5800 Annapolis Road in Bladensburg, Maryland, and the salon was right below, on the ground floor—the business level of the building. It was the perfect setup for a young entrepreneur balancing passion with purpose.

My best friend and roommate, Selena, along with her sister, Tonya Slaughter, played a major role in shaping the next chapter of my story. Tonya was a student at Shaw University and would often drive from North Carolina to Maryland every Thursday with her friends just to get their hair done before heading back in time for ladies' night. Their dedication always impressed me, but I couldn't help worrying about their safety on those late-night drives.

That concern—rooted in love and care—sparked an idea that would change my life. I decided to bring InFlight to them by opening a salon in Raleigh, North Carolina. I had never imagined myself living in the South, yet it became the setting for some of my greatest personal and professional growth. It was there I met my husband, Dr. Connell Covington. Together, we built our businesses, raised two incredible sons, and continued to expand InFlight's reach.

InFlight became more than a salon—it grew into a brand that represented innovation, education, and empowerment. From celebrity clients to high-powered professionals, we welcomed people from all walks of life. Yet, some of our most loyal clients were college students who saw their hair as an extension of their identity. They were bold, ambitious, and eager to make a statement—and InFlight helped them do just that.

Eventually, I expanded into the world of day spas, broadening our services and redefining what beauty and wellness could mean. It was during this next phase that my eyesight began to fade—a turning point that would test everything I had built and everything I believed.

LIFE HAPPENS

At the height of my career, the unthinkable happened—my vision began to change, and my world slowly dimmed. It started with small mishaps, like clipping a mailbox while driving. One moment stands out clearly in my memory: I was behind the wheel of my dream car, a 450 SL Mercedes, when, while pulling into my garage, I suddenly tore the side mirror off. I sat there, stunned. In that instant, I realized it wasn't just the car that was damaged—something within me was changing too.

Seeking answers, I underwent a series of tests at UNC Medical Center. The results revealed a diagnosis of retinitis pigmentosa, a rare inherited eye disease that, at the time, had no cure. The news left me devastated. The doctors couldn't predict how quickly my sight would deteriorate—it could be weeks, months, or years. In the end, it took years, but the gradual loss was just as heartbreaking.

Eye disease had always been part of my family's history—some cases carefully documented, others spoken of only in whispers. My great-grandfather was blind, though no official record ever told his story. My mother, too, lost her sight to glaucoma, a battle that defined much of her life. Yet despite this legacy, blindness was something I never imagined for myself. I was young, healthy, and full of plans—or so I believed. It never crossed my mind that I might one day carry the same burden that had shadowed generations before me.

By 2015, everything shifted in a single appointment. The doctor said the words out loud and entered them into my record: "legally blind." In that moment, I felt my independence slip away. Driving was no longer safe, and the effortless freedom of movement I'd always known was suddenly gone.

The truth is, I had been adapting for a while. I kept building my beauty business and reassured myself that by the time I had to face it fully, a cure would come. But hearing those words—and seeing them written down—made the loss undeniable. What had crept in quietly now stood firm and final.

There was no cure, no treatment, no promise of reversal—as I understood it then. Time couldn't mend it. Money couldn't erase it. Medicine couldn't change the diagnosis. Losing your sight isn't just a physical change—it's an emotional and spiritual unraveling. The journey unfolds in phases: denial, grief, and, eventually, acceptance. I stayed in denial for a long time, fighting against what I already knew deep down to be true.

At first, I refused to face it. I convinced myself it was temporary—that somehow, my vision would return. I avoided learning about accessibility tools or anything that might confirm this new reality because acknowledging it felt like surrender. Sight had always been effortless, something I never questioned until it was gone. Still, I held on tightly to hope—that a cure would come, that science would somehow save me before I lost it all.

But denial always finds a way to reveal itself. I remember one evening at a formal dinner when I accidentally knocked over a glass of red wine. The sound of it spilling seemed to echo across the room, and I could feel every eye on me as I fumbled to clean it up. From that night on, I made a deal with myself—I switched to white wine. It was less of a cleanup and, somehow, less embarrassing.

There were other moments too—times when I'd respond to someone who wasn't even speaking to me or misjudge where a voice was coming from. Each small mistake chipped away at the illusion I had built. Eventually, it became impossible to ignore what was happening, no matter how hard I tried. As a businesswoman, I was always out networking and attending events, connecting with others in my industry. But as my vision declined, navigating rooms filled with people became increasingly difficult. Approaching the people I wanted to connect with was no longer easy—it became almost impossible. The vibrant networking scene that once energized me now left me feeling isolated and disconnected from the world I had worked so hard to be part of.

Eventually, I came up with my own system for handling those awkward moments. I'd have someone quietly point me in the right direction toward whoever I wanted to meet—cane in hand, like a GPS with attitude. Of course, my "navigation" wasn't always perfect. More than once, I'd bump right into someone—sometimes a little harder than I meant to—then flash my best smile and say, "Oh, excuse me! I'm Carolyn Covington... and you are?"

Let's just say a few people met my cane before they met me. But those moments taught me something priceless: if you can't find the humor in your situation, you'll miss half the joy in the journey. As I moved past denial, I entered a deeper and more painful stage—grief. I mourned the loss of something incredibly precious: my ability to see. The grief consumed me, weighing heavily on my mental and emotional health. There were days when the loss felt unbearable, and I couldn't imagine a way forward. It was a period that could have easily led to depression, substance abuse, or other mental health struggles—battles many people face when coping with such profound loss.

Reaching out for support and seeking rehabilitation marked an important turning point in my journey. It was through rehabilitation that I found the strength to accept my blindness, surrounded by mentors who were also blind and understood exactly what I was going through. They shared their own stories of resilience and hope, and their experiences became a source of comfort and courage. Through them, I learned that acceptance doesn't mean giving up—it means choosing to live fully, even when life looks different from what you imagined.

I believe it's essential for everyone to share their stories. When we speak openly about our experiences, we not only help others find inspiration and support but also give ourselves the space to heal and make sense of what we've lived through. Stories have power—they connect us, teach us, and remind us that none of us are alone. One story that deeply reflects resilience and transformation is that of Alice Walker, the author of The Color Purple and The World Has Changed. When she was eight years old, her brother accidentally shot her in the eye with a BB gun. Her family couldn't reach a doctor for days, and by the time she was treated, she had lost sight in her right eye. The scar left her feeling quiet and self-conscious, but in that silence, she discovered something extraordinary—a new way of seeing. The solitude that could have silenced her instead strengthened a voice that noticed what others missed, a voice that would one day move the world.

Walker once wrote, "The most common way people give up their power is by thinking they don't have any." She is living proof of the opposite—and so are many of you reading this. If you've ever been told that your scar or disability is a weakness, remember that strength often begins right there. What was meant to close a chapter in your story can become the reason a new one begins.

Society often overlooks the value and potential of people who are visually impaired because it still tends to view disability through a negative lens. Yet, those with visual impairments are often among the most creative and innovative individuals you'll ever meet or work with. They have the unique ability to see things first in their mind, then bring those ideas to life in ways that help the rest of the world see through their vision.

A NEW VISION WITHOUT SIGHT

That's when God placed a new assignment on my heart—to help the people around me. In 2016, I founded Insightful Visionaries, a 501(c)(3) nonprofit dedicated to empowering people with disabilities. Just as InFlight Salons had filled a gap in the beauty industry for Black women, Insightful Visionaries set out to fill a similar gap for individuals in the disability community—people like me who wanted more out of life and opportunity. As I looked deeper into the landscape of disability support, I realized there were very few programs or business development opportunities designed for the visually impaired. That realization made one thing clear: something had to change.

In building our community, I launched DIVA's Alliance, a network of women with diverse abilities who are Inspirational, Victorious, and Accomplished. Together, we built a sisterhood—one that shared advice, traded professional leads, and celebrated every win, no matter how small. Alongside that connection, we focused on practical growth. We held résumé clinics, pitch practice sessions, and accessible technology tutorials. We also hosted virtual events that reached those who had never before been able to attend in person. Through all of this, we proved a vital truth: inclusion is not an act of charity—it's a design choice that expands opportunity, reach, and results.

My journey has always been rooted in empowerment, innovation, and beauty, so launching CEO Haircare felt like a natural next step. CEO Haircare isn't just a brand—it's a movement dedicated to building confidence from the inside out. I believe every person is the CEO of their own image, fully capable of shaping how they show up in the world—with strength, style, and purpose. Through high-quality, results-driven products and accessible education, CEO Haircare supports not only healthy hair but also healthy ambition. If you have a moment, visit ceohaircare.com—you won't be disappointed.

CORPORATE COVID – HOW THE PANDEMIC CHANGED THE WORLD

When COVID-19 struck, it cast a dark cloud over the world and brought daily life to a halt overnight. Restrictions on movement, access, and independence touched everyone all at once. I called it "Corporate COVID" because once the money chain was threatened, institutions suddenly moved with the urgency the disability community had been pleading for—and rarely received. Within weeks, companies rolled out remote work.

Restaurants perfected curbside pickup. Hospitals, doctors' offices, and treatment centers expanded telehealth. Colleges shifted to virtual classrooms. Even the government found ways to cut through red tape. For the first time, there was widespread empathy for what those of us in the disability community had long experienced. Yet, while the world struggled to adjust, many of us with disabilities found stability amid the chaos. We had already learned how to navigate uncertainty, isolation, and inaccessible systems. Our monthly benefit checks stayed steady when other incomes collapsed. We were the ones who already knew how to live within constraints—and still move forward.

That period revealed a hard truth. When the crisis ended in America, people rushed back to "normal" — or what they called a new normal — and left the lessons behind. The same systems that moved quickly during COVID had, for years, resisted simple changes for people with disabilities. If hospitals could adapt to deliver telehealth within weeks during COVID, they could keep that option available for patients who cannot drive. If restaurants could create curbside pickup, they could maintain accessible ordering and pickup protocols. If offices could run remotely, they could continue offering flexible schedules and accessible technology. Ride-share companies could train drivers on service animal access and stop turning disability rights into customer disputes. These are not minor adjustments; they are the everyday accommodations we requested long before a pandemic made them convenient — or profitable.

At Insightful Visionaries, we turned that moment into structure. We built the IV Resource Hub so people could come to us for services, referrals, and advocacy. We assembled a small multidisciplinary team to handle intake and triage common barriers. Sometimes, we receive calls or referrals about unique issues. For example, a woman once called after a driver refused her ride because of her service dog. We documented the incident, filed a complaint, and connected her with legal support. We've also created business workshops for blind entrepreneurs, fought for funding, won small grants, and survived a federal grant pause. We adjusted budgets, diversified income, and kept the lights on.

But the work doesn't stop with programs or policy—it continues within the community itself. The disability community has work to do as well. We already knew how to live within limits; the world learned it for a time, then tried to forget. Our job is to remember. We must preserve what helped us thrive: telehealth, flexible schedules, curbside access, and accessible tools that made everyday life more inclusive. We can train allies, mentor newcomers, and document our progress so it isn't lost. This isn't about asking for more. It's about holding on to what we proved was possible.

COVID showed the world what we already knew — access helps everyone. Progress moves fast when leaders decide it matters. The question now is whether we will remember. Insightful Visionaries will. We'll keep opening doors, keep telling the truth, and keep building programs that turn imagination into opportunity. Society often underestimates blind people because it sees impairment before it sees talent. Yet the visually impaired are among the most innovative people you'll ever meet. We see ideas in our minds first, then bring them into the world through the sighted eye. That's the vision we live by every day.

Building a more inclusive world starts with something simple — awareness. When we take time to understand one another and respect each person's abilities and contributions, we create a space where people feel seen, valued, and included. That understanding begins with recognizing that vision loss exists on a spectrum. Vision impairment and blindness are classified by several levels, typically based on how much a person's vision differs from normal sight. These categories describe not just total blindness but the range of partial or functional vision loss that affects daily life.

I've learned that empathy isn't passive—it's a daily practice. We live in a culture that often celebrates titles, status, and personal achievement, where "me, mine, my" becomes the rhythm of success. Yet, I've come to believe the real reward isn't found at the top of the ladder but in how we move alongside one another on the way up. Love, care, and humanity will always matter more than perfection.

As a blind woman, I've often been met with questions that once made me feel insulted or frustrated. Questions like, "Why do you need that?" "Why do you do it that way?" or "Why are you doing that if you're blind?" Over time, I stopped hearing those questions as insults and started seeing them as openings. So, when someone says, "You're the busiest blind person I know," I usually respond, "How many blind people do you actually know?" That moment often reveals the truth—the issue isn't me; it's exposure. Most people have simply never been taught how to engage with the blind community respectfully.

So, I teach.

I explain because the goal is to inform. I talk about what respect looks like in real life.

I tell people: speak to me directly, not to the person standing next to me. Hand my card or my change back to me—not to whoever is with me. Understand that blindness doesn't mean I can't communicate for myself. Understand that blindness doesn't mean I can't manage a transaction. And understand that blindness doesn't mean I can't manage me. Also, I'm blind, not deaf—you don't have to shout at me.

In group settings, the harm is usually quieter. Conversations can move around you instead of toward you. People forget to include you because they assume you cannot—or will not—engage. Imagine sitting right there in the room yet feeling invisible. Inclusion isn't just about ramps and railings; it's the habit of bringing people in.

That has not always been easy for me to say out loud. There were nights I cried myself to sleep—not because of blindness itself, but because of what people said, what they assumed, and how quickly they dismissed me or others like me. Those moments hurt. I won't pretend they didn't. But I also realized I couldn't live in that pain. Those tears weren't weakness; they were a washing. They cleared the anger so I could keep showing up with patience instead of bitterness, with purpose instead of shame.

There have been countless nights when I've quietly hummed myself to sleep, comforted by the lyrics of one of my favorite songs. The words have stayed with me, *"If you feel like giving up today, Just remember tomorrow will be a brand-new beautiful day. The sun will rise, and the old things will fade away. You don't have to change a thing about you, you are perfect as you are, you're beautiful."*

To anyone who is blind, visually impaired, or living with any disability and carrying that same weight—your hurt is real. You are not being dramatic. You are not alone. You are allowed to say that something wounded you. You are allowed to ask for better. You are allowed to expect respect. None of that makes you difficult. It makes you human.

Faith has also shaped how I carry my blindness. People sometimes ask if I have ever wanted God to heal my vision. The honest answer is that I had to learn something hard to accept God does not heal everyone physically. A person can pray with full faith and still not receive physical healing—not because they are unworthy, but because sometimes, in that moment, it is God's will. 1 John 5:14 teaches us that we should have confidence when we ask for things according to His will. Sometimes the answer comes in a form we did not ask for. Sometimes the healing is not in the body—it is in the calling. There are even long stretches in the Bible where no physical healing.

are recorded at all. We are not the first generation to live with something that did not go away.

I do not move through this world asking for pity—I move through it asking for awareness and respect. I don't need anyone to lower their voice when talking about disability; I need them to raise their understanding. Inclusion is not charity—it's culture. And culture is built, choice by choice.

Insightful Visionaries exists to educate, advocate, and inspire a deeper understanding of what blind and visually impaired people truly want, need, and value. We focus on advocacy that reshapes perception, helping society learn not just how to treat us with respect, but how to include us meaningfully.

What sighted people often view as obstacles, we see as opportunities—to choose differently, to create change, and to grow stronger. Disability doesn't mean you can't; it simply means you do it differently. Growth begins when we meet ourselves with honesty, self-love, and acceptance.

Our message is simple: dream. Dream beyond what seems possible. Learning to navigate a world built for sight is what makes us more than able. You can do more than you think you can. As I often say in my speeches, "You have to keep dreaming—you have to see yourself doing things before anyone else does."

DREAM BIG, WORK HARD, AND MAKE A DIFFERENCE

Dreaming is the first step toward achieving something remarkable. Each of us carries dreams that reflect our deepest desires and aspirations. Whether it's a career goal, a personal ambition, or a creative pursuit, your dreams are valid—and they're worth chasing.

Everything begins with a single thought that sparks the imagination. That spark fuels passion, and passion ignites motion. It's that steady flame that propels your dream forward.

But dreams aren't just about personal fulfillment; they have the power to reach beyond us and uplift others. Every meaningful dream holds the potential to create positive change in the world. Think about innovators who developed assistive technologies for the blind and visually impaired—like voice assistants that help us navigate the world. Their dreams reached further than personal success; they transformed lives and opened doors for others to thrive.

So, when you chase your dreams, think about how they can serve a greater purpose. Your passion and dedication have the power to inspire others and leave a meaningful mark. Believe in yourself, stay consistent, and never give up—because the work you do can reach further than you imagine.

YOUR PERSONAL PATHWAY TO SUCCESS

Over the past 40 years, I've been blessed with many accomplishments. I've worked as a licensed cosmetologist, instructor, and owner of a salon, spa, and school. I became a hair product manufacturer, mentor, ambassador, advocate, and nonprofit leader. Throughout my journey, I've employed and mentored more than 1,500 people, helping many of them start their own businesses. Balancing a career, raising two sons, and maintaining a strong marriage hasn't been easy, but it's been worth every moment. I am deeply grateful for my husband, who has always been both present and supportive. His belief in me extended beyond our marriage and into every one of my business ventures—past and present. I truly couldn't have achieved any of this without him.

Still, my greatest accomplishment is the legacy I've built—not in spite of my blindness, but because of it. Losing my sight gave me a new perspective on life. It taught me to focus on what truly matters and inspired me to fight for a future where everyone, regardless of ability, has the chance to succeed.

In closing, I've come to understand that my journey has always been about more than sight—it has been about purpose. Blindness may have changed how I move through life, but it has deepened the way I experience it. As an advocate and a voice of hope, I write not only to inspire but also to be inspired. My purpose is to speak to your dreams, to awaken the dreamer within you, and to remind you that resilience is born in the moments when life calls you to begin again. Carry these words with you as gentle affirmations of your strength, your beauty, and the limitless possibilities that unfold when you choose to keep moving forward.

"True vision isn't about seeing with your eyes but feeling with your heart.

Sometimes the most profound insights come not from what we see,
but from what we feel and understand deeply.

In the absence of sight, I discovered a new way to truly see the world.

"Empathy is a language of the heart, and it transcends any physical barriers.

The beauty of life lies not in what we see,
but in how we experience and cherish each moment.

I embrace each day with confidence and grace.

I celebrate my unique perspective and the beauty it brings to the world."

ABOUT THE AUTHOR

Carolyn Marshall Covington is a trailblazing beauty industry leader, entrepreneur, author, and visionary advocate with over four decades of excellence in cosmetology, salon ownership, product development, and business leadership. As the founder of **CEO Haircare**, she has revolutionized hair and scalp wellness through science-based solutions, industry education, and a mission rooted in healthy beauty for all.

With a powerful belief in access, connection, and equity, Carolyn has dedicated her life to opening doors for others. Through **Insightful Visionaries**, her nonprofit organization, she empowers individuals who are blind and visually impaired through workforce readiness, wellness initiatives, arts and culture programs, and inclusive technology. Her commitment to visibility, independence, and community advancement continues to break barriers and redefine what empowerment looks like.

A respected thought leader in inclusive innovation and small-business development, Carolyn has proudly served and collaborated with multiple community-forward organizations, including:

- Mayor's Committee for Persons with Disabilities
- North Carolina Black Women's Entrepreneur Network
- North Carolina Women Business Hall of Fame
- Insightful Visionaries, Founder & Executive Leader

Various State & Community Advisory Boards supporting disability inclusion, entrepreneurship, and wellness.

An author and speaker, Carolyn, transparently shares her journey of faith, resilience, and reinvention — turning personal challenges into purposeful leadership. Her voice strengthens communities, her programs build opportunities, and her story inspires thousands to pursue greatness beyond limitations.

With every chapter she writes, every business she builds, and every life she touches, Carolyn leads with one unshakable truth—*her work is meant to serve others*. This is why all proceeds from her books and speaking engagements booked through info@cmcspeaks.com go to Insightful Visionaries Inc., to support its mission of empowerment.

"Vision is not only what you see, it's what you believe you can become."

ACKNOWLEDGEMENT

First, I give all glory, honor, and thanks to God, who has guided my steps, held my hand through every valley, and lifted me higher than I ever imagined. I am grateful for the journey — the good and the challenging, the victories and the detours — for each experience has shaped me, strengthened me, and prepared me for this purpose.

To every person who has touched my life through love, encouragement, or even adversity — thank you. The lessons learned, the support received, and the obstacles overcome have all helped mold me into who I am today. I am here not in spite of what I have faced, but because of it.

To my family and friends who stood by me, believed in me, and saw my vision even when sight was no longer the path — your unwavering love has been my anchor. Thank you for being my strength when I felt weak and my light when the world seemed dark.

To the blind and visually impaired community, and all who walk their own path toward independence and purpose — you inspire me. This book is for you, and because of you. We are limitless. We are capable. We are powerful in mind, in spirit, and in determination.

And to every reader — thank you for holding these pages, opening your heart, and choosing to see beyond what is visible. May you find inspiration here, and may it remind you that life's journey is not defined by what we lose, but by what we gain, who we become, and how boldly we rise.

With gratitude and unwavering faith,
Carolyn Marshall Covington

Dr. Timothy L. Miles

A WORLD TOO BRIGHT

EARLY LIFE & DIAGNOSIS

From the moment I was born, the world did not welcome me with warmth but with an overwhelming brightness. To most people, light is a comfort—a symbol of clarity and hope. For me, it was an intrusion. My earliest memories are filled with discomfort: squinting at shapes others could see clearly, flinching under sunlight, and watching colors blur and fade into a haze of white and gray.

Rooms had to stay dim, or my vision would shuffle and blur under bright lights, making it hard to move around. If I went to the kitchen for a snack, I had to move quickly. The sunlight pouring in through the window, mixed with the bright yellow and white tiles, strained my eyes, and left me exhausted as I tried to find what I needed. Strangely, I could see more clearly in the kitchen at night. When only the moonlight or the glow from the refrigerator lit the room, my other senses took over. Smell and touch became my guides. My mother, who loved medium-toned colors like blues, greens, and rusts, helped me adjust to light and color without even realizing how much she was teaching me to adapt.

When I was four, my parents were finally given a name for my condition: oculocutaneous albinism. The diagnosis explained not only my light blonde hair and translucent skin but also the unusual way I experienced the world. The nystagmus—the involuntary twitching of my eyes—and my struggle to see details even up close were all part of the same condition. My vision was not gone, but it was limited enough to shape nearly every aspect of my life.

My family's reaction was a mix of concern and fierce protectiveness. My great-grandmother became my first advocate, determined to learn everything she could about albinism. She tried to protect me not just from the harshness of sunlight but also from the harsher judgments of others. My father, however, could not handle the diagnosis—he denied I was his child and left. My mother, quieter but stronger than she realized, showed her love through action. She softened the lighting in our home, guided me through unfamiliar spaces, and learned to recognize the slightest expression on my face when I was struggling. "Timmy, it is too bright. Stop squinting. Where are your shades?" she would say, her voice firm but full of care.

Once, when my mother was both encouraging and gently scolding me to wear my glasses, my great grandmother sat nearby and watched quietly. A few days later, she brought over some strips and lanyards to attach to my glasses so I could keep them on more easily. She insisted I wear them, reminding me that they were meant to help me see where I was going. If she caught me without them, there was always the threat of a spanking, so I quickly learned to keep them on. Like most children, I did not enjoy wearing glasses. I did not want to feel like "four eyes." But for me, it wasn't just about looks—it was about wanting to feel normal, especially since I still had some sight left and a need to take the focus off my skin defect.

My father's departure left a mark that ran deep. His abandonment shaped how I understood family and left behind a sting that words couldn't soften. My lack of pigmentation seemed to embarrass him, creating a distance between us that I could never cross. We never bonded. To him, I was proof that something was wrong—either an accusation of my mother's unfaithfulness or a flaw in his own bloodline. His family had no history of children with disabilities, and from their perspective, I was an outcast. He had fathered two children before me and went on to have seven more with another wife. Even as a small child, I noticed the difference. I remember being just four years old and asking why I didn't have a daddy like my older brother. The conversation was quickly hushed, but the silence said everything.

In the public schools of the 1960s, difference was noticed but rarely understood. My pale hair and constant squint drew stares, and the teasing—"ghost eyes," "half Black, half white"—was more confusion than cruelty. Still, it left its mark. I saw the world differently, literally and figuratively, and for years I thought that difference meant I was broken. Only later did I learn it was a kind of vision all its own. I remember vividly the first time I realized I couldn't read the blackboard like everyone else. I was called on, unable to make out the words, and the kids laughed. The teacher thought I was being "uncooperative" and punished me. The letters blurred together until they were nothing but shapes, and I was left guessing, praying not to be called on again. That moment planted a seed of self-doubt that would take years to uproot.

Still, my family fought for accommodations. I received large-print books, sat at the front of the classroom, and slowly learned to speak up for what I needed—though not without missteps and moments of quiet resentment. Living with albinism and partial sight taught me that difference can be both visible and invisible at the same time. My condition showed in my skin and eyes, but the deeper struggle was hidden: the pounding headaches after hours in bright light, the social distance from always feeling a step behind, and the exhaustion of constantly having to explain myself.

The differences between public school and the school for the blind became more obvious as time passed. Public school had felt hostile and exhausting, both emotionally and mentally. The school for the blind, though, offered better teaching methods and real accommodations because every child there faced some level of vision loss. For the first time, I felt equal—accepted, even. I still missed my family and neighborhood friends, but at the blind school, the teachers didn't laugh at your mistakes or set you up to fail. They encouraged you, supported you, and gave you the space to succeed. Public school had been about surviving socially, not learning. The blind school showed me what education could truly be.

When I was around nine or ten, I officially enrolled there. The transition wasn't easy, but it showed me what resilience could look like. Small moments—like walking across the playground with a friend who naturally slowed down so I could keep pace, or a teacher who quietly gave instructions nearby instead of shouting across the room—became small yet powerful victories. They were the foundation for everything that came next.

LEARNING THE ANGLES OF LIGHT: ADAPTING & COPING IN ADOLESCENCE

By adolescence, I had developed a kind of sixth sense—one that helped me read spaces and people beyond what my eyes could handle. I knew the feel of hallways, the distance between desks, and the tone of voices I could trust. My vision hadn't improved, but I had. I learned how to navigate a fully sighted world with only partial sight.

The latter part of middle school brought a wave of self-awareness—liberating in some ways, but painful in others. I became sharply aware of what I couldn't do, and of what others assumed I couldn't do. Sports were mostly out of reach. I couldn't track a ball fast enough, and even running in a straight line was hard when depth perception wasn't on my side. At that age, physical skill was its own kind of social currency. If you weren't athletic, you had to make up for it by being charismatic, funny, or exceptionally smart.

So, I carved out space through words. I started with journals, then moved to poetry, and eventually to spoken word. Reading and writing became both refuge and rebellion. On paper, I didn't need perfect sight to create something meaningful. I didn't have to compete visually. I just had to feel, imagine, and describe. That outlet reshaped how I saw myself—not as disabled, but as differently equipped.

Technology played its part, too. I used magnifiers, human readers, and devices that could zoom in on text. These tools didn't make me feel "normal," but they made life manageable. Out of necessity, I became skilled at adaptive techniques. I learned the best angles to sit to avoid glare, how to read people's emotions even when their faces blurred, and how to organize my work so I wouldn't fall behind.

Emotionally, it was a turbulent time. Teenagers crave acceptance, and I wrestled with the urge to blend in while knowing I could never completely disappear into the crowd. Friendships were harder to build. Some people couldn't handle the accommodations I needed; others simply didn't know how to connect. The ones who stayed became my anchors—bonds strengthened by empathy rather than convenience.

Through all of it, I built a quiet kind of resilience—not the cinematic kind, but the everyday kind. The kind that pushes you to return to school after being mocked in a hallway. The kind that helps you laugh off a stumble in gym class even when it hurts. I began to own my story instead of hiding from it, and that shift changed everything.

FINDING MY FOOTING: NAVIGATING ADOLESCENCE AND BEYOND

The transition to ninth grade marked a real turning point in my life. As I learned to navigate the hallways of a new school, I also began a deeper journey of self-discovery. For the first time, I started to see myself in a more positive light. I focused on my physical well-being—losing weight, gaining muscle, and even joining the track team. That growing confidence slowly chipped away at the insecurities that had followed me since childhood.

But progress didn't come easily. A constant pull toward home weighed heavily on me, especially because my mother was trapped in an abusive relationship. The thought of being away for long stretches filled me with guilt and worry. I had spent most of my academic life at a school for the blind, and now I felt caught between my newly found independence and the sense of responsibility I carried for my family.

The school for the blind was a paradox. While it separated me from home for much of the year, it also became one of the most positive influences in my life. The house parents, teachers, and fellow students offered care and encouragement unlike anything I had known elsewhere. Two individuals in particular—a houseparent and a teacher—often reminded me that my potential was limitless and that my intelligence could take me anywhere. They checked my homework, offered guidance, and created an environment where learning felt supportive instead of humiliating.

This was a sharp contrast to my public-school experiences, where limited understanding and resources left me feeling isolated and behind. Many teachers at the school for the blind had personal experience with blindness or low vision. They provided accessible materials, encouraged the use of assistive technology, and fostered a genuine sense of community. There, I met others who shared similar challenges, and through their stories, I began to understand my own in a new way.

Moving to the school for the blind had been jarring—a break from the familiar, however imperfect it had been. Yet, it ultimately gave me an education that went beyond academics. I learned self-advocacy, self-awareness, and how to recognize both my strengths and limits. I also developed practical skills like using talking books, writing in large print, and relying on assistive devices. Most importantly, I began shaping an identity that wasn't solely defined by albinism or partial blindness, but by my growing sense of confidence and belonging.

My communication skills grew as well. Encouraged by teachers, I read aloud plays, history passages, or anything that gave me a chance to practice. This not only improved my comprehension but also built my confidence. The positive reinforcement was a stark contrast to the silence or criticism I had known before.

My aspirations began to take shape, too. Inspired by characters like Owen Marshall and Perry Mason, I developed a strong interest in law. Whenever I shared these ambitions, my mother never dismissed them. Her encouragement, combined with the support I received at school, fueled my determination to pursue higher education.

High school still came with its social challenges, but the supportive environment gave me tools to navigate them. The teasing and scrutiny that had defined earlier years gradually eased. Yet anxieties about my mother's situation remained, creating an undercurrent of tension. Looking back, those years were a complex mix of growth and struggle, laying the groundwork for the challenges and triumphs of young adulthood.

EXPANDING HORIZONS: NAVIGATING COLLEGE AND EARLY ADULTHOOD

Leaving the structured environment of the school for the blind and stepping into college felt like walking onto a vast, open plain. The familiar supports were still there, but the responsibility to find them—and to advocate for myself—rested squarely on my shoulders. It was both exhilarating and daunting.

The campus presented immediate challenges. Navigating sprawling grounds with poor lighting or unfamiliar layouts required careful planning and reliance on nonvisual cues. I mapped routes during daylight, walked them repeatedly, and learned to identify landmarks by sound and texture: the feel of cobblestones versus smooth pavement, the distant hum of a building's ventilation system.

Academically, college demanded a different kind of engagement. Disability services provided essential accommodations, such as large-print textbooks and extended time on exams, but the volume of reading and the fast pace of lectures required new strategies. I relied on audiobooks, often listening while following along in print to reinforce comprehension. I worked with note takers and study groups, contributing through verbal explanations and insights shaped by my unique way of processing information.

College also became a crucible for personal growth. I encountered people from backgrounds far beyond my own, with new beliefs, fresh challenges, and alternative ways of seeing. That exposure broadened both my understanding of the world and my sense of where I belonged within it.

Freed from the constant label of "the blind student," I felt more able to define myself by my interests, intellect, and relationships. I joined writing workshops and debate societies, finding communities where my visual impairment was just one facet of who I was.

Two teachers took an interest in me—not just as a student, but as a person with gifts. The first, in communication, helped me discover my ability to speak and present. I learned the craft of oratory, sharing my story both visually and vocally before an audience. In my first speech about vision loss and light, I felt a spark, realizing that my story could empower people to think differently about difference—much like Dr. Martin Luther King Jr.

had when delivering "I Have a Dream" in Washington, D.C. The second teacher, in civil liberties and civil rights, introduced me to the struggles of those denied opportunity because of the color of their skin. It resonated deeply with my own experience of disability discrimination. From that moment, my guiding theme became let the blind be allowed to see.

Socially, there were complexities. Explaining my low vision to new acquaintances required a delicate balance: being honest without letting it dominate every interaction. Awkward moments arose—correcting assumptions, declining activities I couldn't safely do—but there were also meaningful connections with friends who were patient, curious, and willing to understand.

My early career goals still leaned toward law, and I sought internships and volunteer roles to explore that path. I learned to adapt and contribute effectively within my limits. These experiences emphasized the importance of perseverance, clear communication about my needs, and pride in the unique strengths my perspective brought to analysis and problem-solving.

There were rejections and doubts, days when the future felt uncertain. Yet the resilience I had cultivated, along with the support of friends and mentors, kept me moving forward. College was not just about earning a degree; it was about learning to navigate a complex world, building meaningful connections, and shaping a sense of self that was both confident and adaptable.

FINDING MY VOICE: CAREER, ADVOCACY, AND BUILDING BRIDGES

The shift from academia to the professional world brought both challenges and opportunities. My college-nurtured interest in law met the practical demands of work life, where attention to detail, intensive reading, and persuasive communication posed hurdles—but also highlighted where my strengths could shine. Ultimately, my path led me toward Communication Studies and Civil Rights, work that allowed me to combine analysis, storytelling, and advocacy.

Securing my first job required persistence. Interviews became a careful dance: I addressed my visual impairment without letting it overshadow my qualifications. I learned to emphasize adaptability, strong listening skills, and problem-solving—qualities honed by navigating a visually focused world. When accommodations were necessary, I stated them clearly and confidently, framing them not as limitations but as tools for performing at my best.

Once on the job, the learning curve was steep. Dense, visually complex documents demanded innovative approaches. I became proficient with screen readers and magnification software, often working extra hours to ensure thorough comprehension. Not every employer understood accommodations or the obligations of civil-rights laws like Section 504 of the Rehabilitation Act and, later, the ADA. I learned to collaborate openly with colleagues about workflow while contributing in ways that leveraged my auditory strengths and analytical skills.

Within my career, I developed a strong focus on auxiliary aids and assistive technology. I became passionate about ensuring these tools were recognized as essential in education and the workforce—just as necessary as pencils, calculators, or computers. Grants and initiatives, such as those I worked on with IBM and Lotus, helped promote this vision of technology as an equalizer. I also remember mentoring a high school student who had lost confidence because he feared the stigma of wearing glasses. By encouraging him to try contact lenses, he regained his social standing and later told me he would proudly use aids in the future and teach others that looking different doesn't diminish your worth.

There were frustrations—technology that wasn't accessible, misunderstandings that stalled progress. Yet these challenges sharpened my sense of purpose. Living in a world not designed for people with disabilities fueled a passion for advocacy, and my career and cause began to intertwine.

At first, advocacy took the form of informal mentorship: encouraging others with visual impairments entering the workforce, sharing strategies, and connecting people with resources. As my confidence grew, I took on more formal roles—joining disability-rights organizations, speaking on panels, and pushing for systemic change. My training equipped me to analyze discriminatory practices and advocate for fair policies.

One of the most meaningful aspects of this work has been bridging the gap between sighted and visually impaired communities. By sharing practical realities and highlighting capability alongside challenge, I've witnessed perspectives shift. Demystifying disability can be transformative.

As my advocacy deepened, my circle widened. Relationships with people across abilities and disciplines—built on respect and shared purpose—enriched my life and reinforced a sense of belonging. Looking back, this phase was about empowerment: finding my voice not only to advocate for myself but also to amplify the voices of others.

THE TAPESTRY OF CONNECTION: RELATIONSHIPS AND SHARED JOURNEYS

While building a career and navigating low vision, the bonds I formed with family, friends, partners, and mentors became both anchors in rough seas and lights along the path. These connections provided support, perspective, and inspiration, shaping both my personal and professional life.

Family relationships—complicated early on—evolved over time. As I gained independence and began expressing my experiences more clearly, our understanding deepened. My mother, who had once struggled with the unknowns of my condition, became a steady source of pride and support. My siblings, who had found it difficult to understand in childhood, grew into allies, offering both practical help and unwavering care. Those bonds, tested by time and circumstance, became the foundation of belonging.

Friendships, especially those formed at the school for the blind and later in college, carried special meaning. Built on mutual understanding, they required fewer explanations and allowed genuine camaraderie to grow. We shared laughter, moments of rest, and the unspoken experience of navigating a sighted world. These friendships gave us space to release frustrations, celebrate small victories, and simply exist as ourselves.

Relationships, however, were fragile through much of my youth. I spent so much energy trying to earn acceptance in public that, by the time I reached college, I approached new connections with caution. For me, it became less about rejection and more about the curiosity others carried—about culture, gender, religion, and difference. Compared to those questions, my vision felt secondary, though it still shaped how I related to people.

Fortunately, many of my relationships developed naturally through class projects, team debates, and shared interests in social issues. Those genuine points of connection helped me realize I didn't have to chase acceptance; it would come when people saw me for who I truly was. I learned not to rush relationships, but to let them unfold in their own time. Life continues to teach me that each day is enough—and that living it fully, one step at a time, is all that truly matters.

Romantic relationships brought their own joys and challenges. Sharing life with someone who didn't fully understand the daily realities of low vision required vulnerability and patience. It meant explaining the need for specific lighting, the difficulty of navigating unfamiliar spaces, and the fatigue that followed visually demanding days. Partners who met those differences with empathy and curiosity strengthened both connection and trust.

Mentors—both in my field and in advocacy—played an essential role. Their guidance helped me navigate career transitions, confront self-doubt, and grow in my work. Their belief in my abilities often pushed me past comfort and into progress. Those relationships thrived on trust and a shared commitment to making an impact.

Across all these connections, empathy was the common bond. When people took time to understand not only practical limitations but also emotional depth, our relationships deepened. Extending that same empathy toward others' experiences expanded my ability to connect authentically.

A VOICE FOR CHANGE: DEEPENING THE WORK OF ADVOCACY

My advocacy didn't begin with a single defining moment; it evolved gradually, shaped by experience and a growing awareness of systemic barriers. Over time, it shifted from informal acts of support to structured involvement, eventually becoming a central part of both my professional and personal life.

In the early stages, I worked with local businesses to improve accessibility. Navigating dimly lit shops and cluttered walkways had often been frustrating, so I volunteered with a disability-rights organization that conducted accessibility audits and provided recommendations. Seeing how small adjustments—such as rearranging aisles, improving lighting, or adding clearer labels—could transform daily experiences was eye-opening.

Another major focus became the workplace. Drawing on my own experience, I collaborated with human-resources teams to promote inclusive hiring practices and ensure reasonable accommodations. I helped facilitate disability-awareness training sessions and advocated for the adoption of assistive technologies. Often, the greatest obstacle wasn't unwillingness but a lack of understanding about how to build environments where everyone could contribute effectively.

My background in civil rights and Disability Law and policy training became particularly valuable in these advocacy efforts. I participated in discussions about accessibility enforcement and the need to update existing frameworks as technology and workplaces evolved. That work—researching, drafting, and engaging with policymakers—reminded me that meaningful progress depends on both grassroots action and systemic reform.

Education also became a central focus. I worked with schools and colleges to promote accessible materials, assistive technology, and inclusive teaching practices. I often shared personal experiences of feeling marginalized in classrooms that weren't built with my needs in mind, underscoring the importance of early intervention and cultivating inclusion from the start.

One of the most rewarding projects involved a small community college that had long struggled with accessibility. The hallways were cluttered, classrooms lacked proper lighting, and the website was nearly impossible to navigate for students using screen readers. After months of discussions, demonstrations, and persistence, the school finally invested in new technology and staff training. I will never forget the first time a student with low vision walked into class, sat down, and used the adapted materials without needing to ask for help. The expression on their face was quiet yet powerful—a reflection of restored dignity.

Of course, not every effort brought immediate results. There were times when funding was denied or when leaders dismissed accessibility as "too expensive" or "too complicated." Those moments tested my patience but also strengthened my conviction that real progress comes only through persistence. I often thought of my grandmother's fierce determination and my mother's quiet adaptability, realizing that my advocacy was part of a much larger continuum. I wasn't working only for myself but also for those who came before—and those yet to come.

There were both triumphs and setbacks. I witnessed businesses implement changes that transformed customer experiences and saw students flourish in inclusive classrooms. But I also faced resistance and the slow pace of institutional change. Those challenges reaffirmed the importance of persistence and coalition-building. Advocacy is rarely a solitary effort—it depends on partnerships, alliances, and shared commitment across the disability community.

My understanding of disability and inclusion has deepened through this work. What began with my own experience of low vision has evolved into a broader, intersectional perspective—one that recognizes how disability connects with race, gender, and socioeconomic factors. This expanded lens continues to strengthen my commitment to creating equitable solutions for everyone.

REFLECTIONS AND LOOKING FORWARD: A LEGACY OF LIGHT AND INCLUSION

Looking back—from the blurred edges of childhood to the sharper focus of adulthood—I feel both gratitude and purpose. Living with albinism and partial blindness has brought challenges and remarkable growth, shaping me in ways I could never have imagined as the boy staring into an uncertain reflection.

My early years taught resilience. Learning to navigate a visually oriented world with limited sight demanded adaptability, resourcefulness, and trust in senses beyond vision. Those lessons became the foundation of who I am.

Adolescence ushered in self-discovery and adjustment. Writing became my solace, and advocating for my needs began to take root. The school for the blind provided sanctuary, community, and the confidence to recognize and embrace my potential.

College opened my world and clarified who I am. Advocacy grew from that awareness—turning lived challenges into lessons for change, forging meaningful relationships and building communities where inclusion is not a goal, but a shared way of life.

Relationships with family, friends, partners, and mentors have been steady sources of strength and joy. They reminded me of the power of empathy and the shared humanity that connects us beyond difference.

As I look ahead, I imagine a world where accessibility is not an afterthought but a natural expectation. A world where ramps, captions, and tactile signs are designed in from the start. Where children with disabilities enter classrooms and find themselves reflected in both the curriculum and the community. And where technology continues to open doors that once seemed firmly closed.

I am deeply grateful to the people who have walked beside me on this journey—the teachers who whispered encouragement, the friends who slowed their steps so I could keep pace, and the mentors who reminded me that my story mattered. Their belief became my belief, and their kindness became my compass.

"If my life experiences teach anything, it's that difference is not a weakness but a form of strength waiting to be recognized. My hope is that readers, advocates, and allies will carry that truth forward. Together, we can shape a world where inclusion is not an act of charity but a shared commitment to justice, equity, and human dignity.

The legacy I hope to leave is one of light and understanding. Just as I learned to navigate a world that often felt too bright or too blurry, I hope to guide others along their own paths—showing that challenges can be met and that limitations do not define potential. I want my work to nurture empathy, strengthen inclusion, and inspire future generations to build a more just and accessible world.

My life reflects resilience, connection, and the transformative power of advocacy. From confusion to clarity of purpose, I have lived through shades of light—learning, adapting, and striving to create a brighter future for myself and others. I carry with me the lessons of the past, the strength of the present, and an unwavering hope for what lies ahead.

ABOUT THE AUTHOR

Dr. Timothy L. Miles, a native of Forsyth County, North Carolina, earned his Master of Arts from the University of North Carolina at Chapel Hill, with dual concentrations in African and Afro-American Studies and Communication Studies. With over thirty years of experience in the human services field, he has developed innovative assistive technology training programs and produced the cable-access program Conversation Pieces.

A passionate advocate for accessibility and inclusion, Dr. Miles served as President of the Orange County Disability Awareness Council (OCDAC), which honored him with an Honorary Doctorate in 1999. His contributions to disability advocacy and education have been recognized with numerous awards, including the Governor's Volunteer Service and Lifetime Achievement Award (1997) and the Trailblazer Award from Insightful Visionaries.

As a person with disabilities, Dr. Miles combines lived experience with professional expertise to advance ADA compliance and equity, promoting accessibility as a fundamental civil right.

ACKNOWLEDGEMENTS

This short story is written in loving memory of my three mothers and two great college educators and mentors.

"Keep your face to the sunshine and you cannot see a shadow."

— Helen Keller

"You don't need sight to walk in purpose."

—Unknown

Adelaide Tabb

DEDICATIONS

I would like to dedicate this book to all those who have ever felt alone. Please know—you are *never* truly alone. There is always someone nearby who cares, someone willing to help you find the light. Just hold on a little while longer; brighter days are ahead.

I also dedicate this book to individuals living with disabilities across this nation and around the world. While many groups have fought for equality, our voices are often left unheard, our contributions overlooked. Too often, we are mocked, discredited, or told to simply be grateful for whatever we are given. To that, I say—no more.

Whether facing racial or ethnic discrimination, sexism, or classism, people with disabilities have long been treated as society's castaways. But we are not victims—we are visionaries, dreamers, doers, and advocates. For those who cannot speak, I promise to continue using my voice to speak up and stand tall on your behalf.

I would also like to thank those who doubted me or believed I wouldn't succeed. I see you—and I thank you. Because God often uses those doubts, and the strength of my community, to fuel my determination and drive every dream forward.

Lastly, I dedicate this book to my son, Eli. You are the sunshine in my darkest days and the laughter that carries me through the hardest moments. You are my greatest accomplishment. Thank you for your smile, your optimism, and your carefree spirit—you make me whole and give my life meaning.

And a special thank you to Martin Ross for believing in me, encouraging me daily, and reminding me to use the gifts God has given me to be great. Thank you for being both my pianist and my friend.

Kebra C. Moore |

LIVING BY FAITH AND NOT BY SIGHT

THE JOURNEY BEGINS

When we are born, none of us know what paths our lives will take or what challenges we will have to face. What I have learned is that, whatever journeys life brings, we are born fully equipped with the tools to endure them. It's easy to say that after you've lived through many trials and reached your forties. But when you're in the middle of hardship—when the weight of life feels too heavy to carry—there are moments when you truly don't know if you'll make it through. It's only after the storm has passed that your testimony begins to take shape. When we're young, we rarely stop to evaluate our circumstances, nor do we yet have enough life experience to see them clearly.

As you read this part of my story, I want you to understand that the wisdom I now share came through time, endurance, and many storms. It is from surviving those difficult seasons that I have learned how to bring light to others who may still be walking through their own darkness.

Imagine being eighteen years old and looking back on your life. Most people would tell you that you don't know anything of real value because you haven't lived long enough. Many adults tend to minimize young people's experiences, overlooking how much they've learned from their struggles. Few ever stop to ask what shaped their perspective or how certain moments influenced the way they think and feel.

So, imagine how I felt when every adult in my life dismissed my feelings and experiences. I was often seen as overly dramatic, as if my life were some kind of soap opera playing out in real time. It didn't matter what I was going through—whenever I opened up about my challenges or shared even small glimpses of my reality, I was brushed aside. And this began long before my vision loss.

TRUST BROKEN

I was fourteen when I realized I couldn't depend on adults to protect me, listen to me, or help me make sense of what was happening. That realization changed everything. I withdrew, became skeptical of people's intentions, and found it hard to let anyone close. Trust slipped away, and family support was nowhere to be found. How does a young girl make it to eighteen after everything she's been through? Let's take a small journey into one of God's miracle stories—and you can tell me what you think.

After being removed from my biological mother's care before the age of two, I was placed with my father's first wife and my half-sister, who was thirty years older than me. Everything felt strange—new and frightening. One of my earliest memories is of my sister, who would have been thirty-four at the time, sharing grapes with me in her room. I sat on her bed watching television beside her. When I finished eating, she became angry and told me she wouldn't share anything else with me because I "ate and ran."

She went on and on about how selfish I was and how rude it was for me to eat her food and leave. At that age, I didn't understand what our relationship would become, but looking back now as an adult, it was giving clear bully energy. By the time I was four, I was already afraid of my sister because of how she treated me. Of course, most children that age think anyone who scolds them is mean, but as I grew older, I realized this went far beyond that. It wasn't just mean or selfish—it was cruel. We'll move through these events in order, so I can give you a clearer picture of what happened and help you better understand my journey.

THE SILENCE I WAS FORCED TO KEEP

I was only three years old when I experienced my first inappropriate sexual encounter with a male family member. After that, the abuse continued—by both men and women—until I was twelve. At twelve, I finally told my stepmother what had been happening. That was also the first time I remember feeling real fear and hatred. She told me I had to go to every adult in our home and admit that I had lied about the abuse. The man I had accused was my sister's live-in boyfriend. My stepmother warned that if I didn't take back what I said, my father would be harmed. In my young mind, that was the worst thing I could imagine. My sister made it clear that if anything happened to her boyfriend, she would call the police on everyone in the house that night. To be fair, I don't know if my sister would have actually implicated our father, but I couldn't take that chance.

When I re-entered the room where my family was waiting, I told everyone that I had misunderstood my sister's boyfriend's actions—that he and I had only been playing. Robert, the offender, even went so far as to pick me up in his arms to prove that nothing inappropriate had happened. In that moment, I understood what humiliation felt like, and it was also the moment I felt hatred for the first time. I made a vow to myself that I would never share anything so personal again. I began to believe that adults couldn't be trusted—at least not with my safety. I started relying on information I gathered from school, television, and the streets to learn how to protect myself. By then, I had already endured sexual abuse from both men and women—some family members and others family friends. Trust became something I could no longer depend on, and that belief stayed with me through most of my adult life. I was also experiencing food insecurity.

Missing school was never an option because it meant missing the one guaranteed meal of the day. It wasn't that my stepmother refused to feed me, but our home was overcrowded, and there was rarely enough food to go around.

My stepmother always made sure the children ate first, but when there was no food in the house to begin with, there was nothing to give. I wore clothes that didn't fit—hand-me-downs and pieces from the local secondhand store that made me too embarrassed to go outside. What could I do as a child? Who could I call? In my mind, there was no one. I tried talking to my dad about the abuse, but he thought it was just sibling rivalry. He would often tell me to stop arguing and try to get along. I could've done that—if it had truly been a simple disagreement. But how do you make peace with someone who's thirty years older than you and believes they're your mother?

I never respected my sister. There were times I even wished she would die, just so I could have peace in my life. Looking back, I believe my stepmother—who was my sister's biological mother—used her as the disciplinarian. My stepmother was older and tired, and after a while, she simply didn't want to be bothered with me. This dynamic caused deep tension between my sister and me, so much so that we don't speak to this day.

The cruelty I experienced from my sister changed me forever. The mere thought of her still brings anxiety and takes me back to a part of my life that holds few good memories. What makes it worse is that she has never apologized for what she did—nor does she believe she did anything wrong. Even so, I've learned to make peace with my life and accept the changes I had to make because of her.

DREAMS AND DARKNESS

So, I know by now you're probably asking yourself, what kind of book is this? I promise, if you hang in there with me, it'll all make sense. After twelve years of sexual abuse, I had to learn how to believe in myself because that lesson wasn't going to come from my home. I was often put down for the things I liked or wanted to do. I remember being around ten years old when I was beaten for using typing paper to build a little home and furniture for my dolls. My sister came into my room yelling about how messy it was and how no one would want to be around a pig. I tried to explain that I was just playing, but it didn't matter. She slapped me across the face and made me clean up my things. That kind of treatment happened often. I kept notebooks filled with my writings—stories, poems, and songs—but they were read without my permission, criticized, and thrown away. Sometimes I was forced to toss them myself.

By the time I turned twelve, I had been called every name in the book—even ones that would make the devil ashamed. By the time I entered high school, when people tried to make fun of me, there was nothing they could say that would hurt my feelings anymore. I'd already heard worse. I hated being around my so-called family and wanted to move in with my dad and his second family. But that never happened, for reasons I still don't understand to this day. At twelve, I had already started making plans for my future. Every Thursday night at eight o'clock, I would sit and watch The Cosby Show and A Different World. I got lost in those shows, imagining that when I turned eighteen and graduated from high school, I'd move onto a campus at a historically Black college and never return to the hellhole I called home. What I didn't know then was that God had other plans for me.

WHEN THE LIGHT WENT DIM

At the age of twelve, I lost seventy percent of my vision in less than two weeks. There was no cure. The scariest part was realizing I might never be able to go off to college and finally leave that miserable life behind. I was terrified that I would have to live with those people much longer than I wanted. After that, I threw myself into everything. I became an overachiever—academically and in every other area of my life. I felt I had to be the best at everything to increase my chances of being accepted into more exclusive places, places that might give me the opportunity to build my own life without the family from hell.

Still, I felt completely alone. My biological mother was in and out of my life, my dad had remarried, and my stepmom didn't want me around. I rarely saw my grandparents. There was no one I could depend on or turn to for advice. Most of the time, if I didn't know what to do, I simply did nothing. After losing my vision, I got involved in every sport and after-school activity I could—anything that kept me out of the house a little longer. I never saw my vision loss as something that would stop me. I just kept trying everything. This period of my life included getting an after-school job at Hometown Buffet as a waitress, running track for my high school, singing, performing on the dance team, joining the school flag team, and even getting married right after graduation. I tried everything I could to escape the miserable existence I called life. There were times I felt so hopeless that I tried to take my own life twice—but God clearly had other plans for me.

Through all of this, music and singing remained my lifeline. There was nothing I loved more than singing. It was the only thing my stepmother allowed me to do freely, without punishment or criticism. I could sing as loudly and as long as I wanted, and I'd never get into trouble for it. Even when my sister tried to make me stop, her mother would step in and tell her to leave me alone. I spent countless hours singing and writing songs, often losing myself in daydreams that always led back to music. I wanted desperately to learn to play the piano, but we simply couldn't afford it. Things began to shift when I reached high school. My English teacher, Dr. Gall, saw something in me and decided to help. She paid for me to attend the historic Karamu House in Cleveland—a theatre known for launching the careers of actors like Halle Berry, Terrence Howard, and Ruby Dee. For the first time, someone outside my family believed in me, and that belief changed everything.

As I mentioned earlier, I had become an overachiever, always competing with the highest-performing student in my classes to motivate myself to strive for excellence. Math had always been one of my strongest subjects, and in 1996, my math teacher, Ms. Chue, recommended that I compete in a national math competition in Washington, D.C. Unfortunately, I never got the chance to go because my stepmother wouldn't allow me to participate. Several teachers even offered to help pay for the trip, but due to the ongoing abuse in our home, my stepmother was afraid I might tell someone what was really happening. She feared that both she and her daughter would end up in prison. I was denied the opportunity to pursue my dreams because of the incompetence and fear of the adults who were supposed to protect me. Still, even then, I was determined to find a way to escape that home and build a better life for myself.

THE ESCAPE THAT WASN'T

Once I got married, I thought things would finally start looking up for me. Yes, I was young, but I wasn't naïve. I knew that because my ex-husband and I had married so early, we were bound to face some challenges. Still, I tried to give our relationship the best chance to survive by helping him understand what I had endured my entire life. One day, while we were still dating, he came over to visit. My stepmother asked him to take out the trash, and I immediately jumped in, offering to do it myself. I only offered because I didn't want it said later that I was lazy or that a visitor had to do my chores. As soon as he stepped outside, my stepmother turned on me. She started yelling, calling me every name she could think of—stupid, lazy, and worse. She said she didn't even know why he wanted to be with me in the first place. Her words cut deep, and even though I tried to hide how much they hurt, they stayed with me. What my stepmother didn't know was that my boyfriend—who would later become my husband—had been standing at the top of the stairs. He heard everything.

He denied hearing anything when she questioned him, and we went on to prepare for dinner. Later that night, I told my ex-husband that I would understand if he didn't want to continue our relationship. I knew my family was a lot to handle, and dating someone with vision loss might not have been what he imagined for his first marriage. He assured me that he loved me and would never leave. But, needless to say, he eventually did. After six and a half years together, our marriage ended. I believe he thought he was doing the noble thing. I hold no grudges against him, but his departure only deepened my distrust in people—especially after he left me homeless. That period of my life was dark. Still, I pushed forward. I enrolled in college after finishing community college, moved onto campus at my four-year university, and graduated in 2004 with my Bachelor of Arts degree. The very next year, I became pregnant with my son.

When I met my son's father, he told me he had never been married and didn't have any children. That turned out to be a lie. I later discovered he had a wife and two little girls. I found all this out when I was already more than four months pregnant.

After he decided I wasn't worth it, I raised my son on my own. I refused to let him take away my freedom, keep lying about his family, or have any more of his children. He told me that if I wouldn't have more children with him or continue seeing him while he was married, he would move on and never come back.

In nearly twenty years, I've seen my son's father fewer than twenty times. I raised my son alone, giving him the life I had always wished for myself. In 2009, I returned to college to earn my Master's degree in Nonprofit Administration and graduated in December 2012. School had always been a safe place for me — somewhere I could grow, learn, and heal. College also gave me opportunities to keep performing; I participated in three plays and held my first solo concert in June 2005.

A PURPOSE REVEALED

Having my son was the best part of my younger years. At twenty-seven, he gave my life purpose — especially after I had tried to take my own life twice. Through him, I learned patience. He showed me what real love is and taught me how to give it without conditions. I knew I had to be for my son what I had never experienced from my mother. My dad loved me deeply — I was a daddy's girl — but it's different when that love comes from a father instead of a mother. I was rough around the edges and demanded respect, while also giving it in return. My father always taught me not to start confrontations but to handle them if they came my way. He talked to me about boys and warned that many only wanted sex, not love or a real relationship, especially if I became pregnant at a young age. In short, he taught me to fight and never give up. He worked hard every day, came to my rescue whenever I needed him, and became one of the greatest influences in my life — second only to my grandmother.

The irony is that my father and grandmother were complete opposites. My grandmother was deeply religious and never denied her faith in the Holy Trinity, while my father ran a gambling house on weekends. After his second divorce, he often had a younger woman around. Even though they were so different, I found comfort in talking to my dad about life. He always told me the truth — never sugar-coating things or pretending they were something sweet when they weren't.

By now, with everything I've shared, you're probably wondering when my life began to turn around. Honestly, it happened when I had my son. It wasn't easy, but holding a brand-new baby — my baby — softened my heart in ways I never expected. I would sit and watch him sleep, take pictures of him throughout the day, and play with him until we both fell asleep. Even on the days when I didn't feel like being present, I knew I had to be. I had to sing songs even when they got on my nerves. I had to pretend when I didn't want to, and stop what I was doing, even when I was right in the middle of something, if he needed me. Through my son, God showed His faithfulness to me. He revealed His love, His patience, and every one of the Fruits of the Spirit. It was through my commitment to my son that the Lord revealed His commitment to me. I became the person my son needed, even though I was still broken inside and battling feelings of abandonment. By that time, I had been in therapy twice, trying to live beyond my trauma.

Although I was no longer physically alone, I still felt lonely, isolated, and hurting. I eventually took time to pause and look back over my life, realizing that nothing I had experienced was by accident. After having the same dream about my baby for three nights in a row, I finally understood that my son's life was blessed by God — and so was mine. Everything I had endured had a purpose.

THE POWER WITHIN

If there's one thing I would want the world to see, it's the resilience people show when they're up against the wall. I want others to understand that your future isn't determined by your hardships or trials, but by how you allow them to shape you into the best version of yourself—for you and for others. The power we each hold to impact the lives around us is immense. What I've learned is that none of us choose the paths we'll face once life begins, but we do have total control over how we let those experiences influence us. If I had chosen to respond negatively to my upbringing, I would've robbed myself of countless opportunities. You may be asking, how does a child avoid letting their experiences define them as an adult? The truth is—you can't. Living with trauma isn't something anyone chooses; it's something you choose to live through. As we grow into adulthood, it becomes our responsibility to seek healing through therapy, family support, and prayer.

I am deeply grateful for my grandmother's prayers. It was through her intercession that I was protected while enduring my hardships. What I want readers to remember is that your power lies within. As painful as my childhood was, I wouldn't change it—because changing it would mean changing who I've become. I've learned that, no matter what my experiences might have been, the lessons they carried have shaped me into the person I am today. Through both my son and the Most High, I've learned patience, faithfulness, kindness, and love. As I poured into my child, I realized that God was also pouring into me. Through me, my son came to experience the love of God. By necessity, I had to strengthen my relationship with God, because where else could I have received such on-the-job training in love, care, and protection? I've also learned that I've accomplished what I have largely because I learned to rely on myself.

I want others to understand that true power comes from within. While it would be wonderful to grow up with two loving parents and strong friendships, many of us don't experience that until adulthood—when we finally have the ability to change our children's lives for the better. I have found so much joy in watching my son grow and develop into the young man he is today, imperfections and all. Those of us who have overcome our struggles have a responsibility to reach out and help others who need to be seen, heard, and encouraged as they continue their own journeys. We must show through our lives that anything is possible when you believe in yourself and your dreams. By allowing others to witness us thrive—not just survive—we pour life into their spirits. We have the rare and beautiful opportunity to take what was once broken and create something whole and extraordinary.

A MESSAGE TO THE WORLD

I also want people to understand that not everyone with a disability was born with one. It can take just one accident, one misdiagnosis, one fall, or one wrong move to change a person's life completely. I want others to realize that everyone faces challenges—some are simply easier to hide than others. We should always treat people with dignity and respect, because the universe is watching, and karma has a long memory. People living with disabilities lead full lives, build successful careers, and make meaningful contributions. Even when we don't see the rainbow often, we can still carry a bit of sunshine to brighten someone else's day.

While I was in school, no one did my work for me. I studied, wrote all my papers, took my own exams, and prepared my own presentations. It may have taken me twice as long, but I got it done. I've accomplished many things in life—singing, acting, designing clothes, and travelling—but the most important role I've ever had is being a parent. Watching my son grow into a man fills me with pride and gratitude for my own little piece of heaven.

Kebra C. Moore |

TO THE CHURCH

The final audience I want to address is the church and other religious institutions. Historically, people have said that those living with disabilities are cursed by God—but I challenge that notion. Nowhere in any sacred text does it teach us to harm or reject someone because of a disability or illness. God calls us to love everyone, even our enemies. I am often approached by people who ask if hands can be laid on me or if prayers can be offered to heal my eyes. My response is simple: pray that I hear the voice of the Lord when He speaks. Pray that my heart remains open and does not harden because of life's challenges. And most importantly, thank God that I have made it this far. We should never question someone's spirituality simply because we do not understand why God has allowed them to experience their disability.

To drive that point home even further, the simple fact that any of us get up each day—go to work or school, care for our families, run businesses, preach, and teach—is proof that we believe. Every morning, we rise without knowing what or who the day will bring, yet we expect good things. We wake up wanting to make a positive difference in the world. I know that I wake up each day excited about whatever surprises it may hold. I don't need anyone questioning my faith because I face the world every single day—living by faith, not by sight. I am like the birds. I can't see what's beyond three feet in front of me. I can't read printed materials, and yes, I depend on others for certain kinds of help—but I wake up every morning without worrying about who will take care of me because I know I'm already taken care of. I stand tall. I stand strong. I hold my head high, knowing that I am perfect with all my imperfections.

I live by faith—not by the sight of the world, but by the sight of my God in heaven. I trust Him to bring me safely through harm and danger. I trust Him to open doors so I can work and provide. I trust that He has never forgotten me—and I can prove that He hasn't. I'm standing here today, healing and thriving with each passing day. I live by faith, not by sight. This brief glimpse into my life is by no means a full account of my hardships. Some of the others may have been even more devastating, but I don't want anyone to focus only on the darkness. I want them to remember the champion that was born from within it.

THE FORCE BEHIND THE STORM: KEBRA C. MOORE, VISIONARY

Kebra C. Moore is a No. 1 Amazon bestselling author of four compelling novels, the founder and CEO of Welcome To The Storm Publishing, and the visionary behind the powerful anthology series, Our Power – The Anthology. A passionate advocate, creator, and entrepreneur, Kebra uses every platform available to uplift and amplify the voices of women who are too often overlooked—especially those within the disability community.

A graduate of Claflin University, Kebra earned her degree in Music Education and has long blended her love for the arts with her commitment to advocacy. She is also an accomplished singer-songwriter; her original song *"He'll Make a Way"* was featured in the documentary *Becoming Barack*, chronicling the early life of President Barack Obama.

After surviving a life-altering spinal cord injury, Kebra made the decision to transform her pain into purpose. She realized that far too many stories from women with disabilities, particularly Black women, were being silenced or forgotten. Determined to change that, she launched *Our Power – The Anthology*, a collection built to showcase real, raw, and resilient voices from across the country.

Following these impactful releases, **Volume IV**, *Our Power – The Anthology: What I Wish the World Could See*, will be released in **November 2025**. This powerful installment shines a light on authors who live with visual impairments and other unseen disabilities, offering the world a rare and authentic look through their lens of strength, perseverance, and purpose. Each story is a heartfelt reflection of resilience—an invitation to see beyond physical limitations and into the boundless power of the human spirit.

The series will continue with ***Our Power – The Anthology, Volume V: Beyond the Spectrum***, which will explore the voices and experiences of individuals within the neurodiverse community. Through these stories, readers will gain deeper insight into the beauty of different ways of thinking, learning, and leading. Together, these volumes continue the legacy of *Our Power*—a movement that uplifts, educates, and inspires by showcasing the extraordinary power that lies within every journey.

Outside of publishing, Kebra is the creator of the Tropical Storm Collection, a vibrant beauty line known for its bestselling matte lipsticks and the eyeshadow palettes. Her goal with every product is to help women feel bold, beautiful, and seen.

Kebra has been married for over 25 years and is the proud mother of two grown sons. She is also an active and financial member of Delta Sigma Theta Sorority, Incorporated, through which she continues to mentor, serve, and support communities in need.

In the spring of 2026, Kebra will expand her mission even further by launching an 8-week course titled *"Start Your Own Publishing Company,"* where she will guide aspiring entrepreneurs through the fundamentals of building a fast-paced, sustainable publishing business, from forming an LLC and securing ISBNs, to formatting, distribution, marketing, and beyond.

Her journey is one of resilience, purpose, and undeniable power. Through every storm, she has found a way not just to survive—but to lead, create, and elevate others along the way.

To learn more about publishing your book or enrolling in Kebra's 8-week course, visit w2tspublishing.org.

www.ingramcontent.com/pod-product-compliance
Lightning Source LLC
Chambersburg PA
CBHW050652160426
43194CB00010B/1914